AWARENESS and WISDOM in Addiction Therapy

The In-depth Systemics Treatment of Mental-somatic Models

Leo Gürtler, Urban M. Studer, & Gerhard Scholz

Vipassana Research Publications

Vipassana Research Publications
an imprint of
Pariyatti Publishing
www.pariyatti.org

© 2011 Leo Gürtler, Urban M. Studer, & Gerhard Scholz | Karlsruhe, Germany; Winterthur, Switzerland

Illustrations © 2011 Gürtler, Studer & Scholz

ISBN: 978-1-681723-42-6 (softcover)

ISBN: 978-1-928706-34-2 (ePub)

ISBN: 978-1-928706-39-7 (Mobi)

ISBN: 978-1-928706-64-9 (PDF)

Library of Congress Control Number: 2010924033

Translation from the German: Ernst Arnold, Judy Caughley, Leo Gürtler, and Luke Matthews

Cover design: Leo Gürtler

Gürtler, Studer, & Scholz

Awareness and Wisdom in Addiction Therapy
The In-depth Systemics Treatment of Mental-somatic Models

The Authors

Dr. Leo Gürtler, psychologist, PhD in educational sciences, systemic coach and therapist, freelancer, therapeutic research at start again. leog@anicca-vijja.de

Dr. Urban M. Studer, mathematical physicist (ETH Zürich), systemic coach and therapist, therapeutic researcher and therapeutic leader at start again, leader of internal case management at the Swiss Federal Railway (SBB). umstuder@sunrise.ch

Dr. Gerhard Scholz, sociologist, systemic coach and therapist, founder and chief executive officer at start again (www.startagain.ch) and 'mensch und organisation' (m&o, www.muo.ch). g.scholz@muo.ch

Realization and Practice

des Wann, beim Wie des Was, im Wo

Abstract

This essay explores the In-depth Systemics treatment and its impact on the structural modification of mental-somatic models (patterns of thinking, feeling, and doing), and, as an example, addiction therapy at start again, a professional drug therapy center in Switzerland. In-depth Systemics is an approach, based on compassion and empathy, to help other people help themselves. By making use of a systematic and methodologically controlled method, individuals come to question their own mental models and gradually dissolve them. This serious undertaking aims at fostering personal development and maturity. The focus is clearly on self-help assistance—i.e., assisting others to realize their autonomy. The profound confrontation of one's own mental models (e.g., one's own addiction) is realized by means of the transformative practice of Ānāpāna-sati and Vipassanā meditation—awareness and wisdom. The application of the In-depth Systemics approach, however, is not limited to professional addiction therapy nor to the field of pathological deviances or psychological disorders. As well as helping people with mental problems, it can also assist those seeking personal growth—both have to transcend their mental boundaries. Indepth Systemics can thus be applied in other fields and contexts: health care, case management, coaching, maximizing athletic ability, personal leadership, etc.—as long as its inherent logic is adopted properly.

Foreword

Drug addiction inflicts immense damage in contemporary society. Individual addicts suffer greatly themselves, and the pain spreads to their family and friends who care about them. Thus, in human terms, the cost of addiction is high, and the need for more effective treatments remains urgent.

Affective neuroscience studies in recent decades have produced evidence to suggest that the brain mechanisms of addiction are complicated and deep. The pleasure of drugs and the distress of withdrawal are important factors, but there is more. In at least some individuals, there may be near-permanent changes in brain systems that mediate subtle but powerful psychological processes of craving. Some of these processes may be so deep as to act essentially unconsciously, under the surface of what is accessible to self-awareness. Therefore motives for taking drugs may remain confusing even to the person who takes those drugs, and the stresses of modern life may potentiate these processes, contributing to exacerbation of craving and relapse.

Gürtler, Studer, and Scholz wrestle here with the practical issues of treatment that arise from such neural underpinnings, and describe the therapy they have developed to try to help addicts abstain more successfully. To gain greater self-awareness of impulses and cravings may be a step toward gaining greater autonomy in the control of action, and escape from the need to react blindly to a craved drug when its cues are encountered in dangerous situations. Greater autonomy and improved abilities to resist impulses and cravings are likely to be of value in helping an addict emerge from the destructive patterns of addictive behavior. Programs such as they describe may be among the useful steps that addicts can currently take, given the present limits on science, to escape the cycle of addiction that imposes such a great cost.

Kent C. Berridge, July 12, 2009
(Professor of Psychology and Neuroscience,
University of Michigan, USA)

Contents

Whatever the case is — is the case.

Verdict of the In-depth Systemics

On the concept of the In-depth Systemics approach

The[1] In-depth Systemics approach[2] is a specific form of continuous effort to help others process dysfunctional mental-somatic models (patterns of thinking, feeling, and doing). It is based on the ancient wisdom that (self-) deceptions will be dissolved if they are countered by direct experience rooted in systematic self-observation by applying the techniques of mindfulness and wisdom meditation. This wisdom refers to the realizations of the historical Buddha, Siddhattha Gotama, who lived in India more than 2500 years ago.

In this essay we present the In-depth Systemics approach and its practical implementation through the example of in-depth work with addiction. In-depth Systemics is, however, effective not only for addictions. It can be applied in a multiplicity of professional contexts[3] (e.g., diverse occupations in health services, case management, training and coaching high-level employees, learning communities, athletics, etc.). Employing the approach in these other areas is not a matter of simple transfer, but requires applying certain principles systematically, working with one's own mental-somatic models and adapting these to the specific context in each case. To keep this essay short and simple we present the application of the In-depth Systemics approach in the area of drug addiction only. The text intends, however, to open up a vision beyond drug addiction, a vision that was formed during our many years of practical institutional experience and scientific evaluation. We hope this vision will reach, equally, meditators in their efforts to develop a more professional approach to their work, and professionals in their efforts toward integration of their own meditation experience.

Notes

1   The authors wish to thank Ernst Arnold, Judy Caughley, and Luke Matthews for their support in translating and editing this essay. Their efforts strongly enhanced its quality. We also want to thank all the clients and co-workers, past and present, who helped us develop the In-depth Systemics approach.

   A (previous) German version of this essay was originally published in Anderssen-Reuster, Ulrike (2007). *Achtsamkeit in Psychotherapie und Psychosomatik. Haltung und Methode* [Mindfulness in Psychotherapy and Psychosomatics: Composure and Methods], pp.113–135. Stuttgart, New York: Schattauer. It is freely available at www.tiefensystemik.net through the courtesy of Schattauer Publications.

2   This essay is a shortened version, encapsulating the essence of an extensive book on the same topic written by the authors in German— *In-depth Systemics. Volume 1. Conduct of Life and Theory: Finding a Way out of Addiction.* ISBN 978-3-86991-030-7. Münster: Monsenstein & Vannerdat. Additional information is available at www.tiefensystemik. net.

3   The development of In-depth Systemics within various professional contexts is mostly carried out by the company 'mensch und organisation' (m&o, www.muo. ch), Winterthur, Switzerland.

Chapter

2

Yaṃ kiñci vedayitaṃ,
tam pi dukkhasmiṇti. (Whatever sensations one
experiences, all are suffering.)

Tipiṭaka, M III, 208

Introduction

Addiction is one of the most impressive variants of the loss of functional autonomy in the life of the individual. Rarely are the social descent, the continual injuries to the body, the inability to utilize the potential for autonomy, etc., so obvious. When treating an addiction, one constantly faces the challenge of arranging appropriate basic conditions that will actually permit addicted persons to have experiences that lead them to disentangle themselves gradually from the addiction, and at the same time let them recognize that a purely intellectual insight into their addiction is not sufficient for engaging mentally at a deeper level. This essay describes a combined approach in which the meditation teachings of the Buddha are integrated with sociological as well as psychological perspectives and neurobiological understanding. The key ingredient, Vipassanā meditation, is highlighted as the essential instrument for engaging the deeper layers of addiction. This modus operandi originated at the Swiss addiction therapy center start again,[4] which has successfully applied In-depth Systemics treatment since 1992. There the concept is based on the combined use of skillfully interwoven case-specific addiction therapy, systemic couples and family therapy, self-help, and the meditation techniques of Ānāpāna-sati and Vipassanā .

Understanding the In-depth Systemics concept requires a basic introduction to the typical aspects of the logic of addiction as a form of impaired autonomy (see section 6.2 for more details on the concept of autonomy). From this we can discern the consequences for therapeutic practice. First we present relevant models for explaining addiction. Then the practical perspective of Vipassanā is underlined, followed by a short outline of the factors necessary for successful recovery from addiction. The integrated concept of start again, namely the In-depth

Systemics approach, is described next. An extensive case study of the effectiveness of the therapeutic program is available (Studer, 1998) from which we quote the most important results. We then formulate hypotheses about the principles of recovery using, as examples, certain cases from a catamnesis investigation that one author (Gürtler) carried out (Gürtler, Studer, and Scholz, 2010). Finally, some fundamental considerations are given to the place of relapse and compliance in addiction therapy.

Notes

4. www.startagain.ch

Addiction is more than mere drug use. It is defined specifically as a compulsive pattern of drug-seeking and drug-taking behavior that takes place at the expense of most other activities.

Addiction
T.E. Robinson & K.C. Berridge

Foundations — about the logic of addiction

*I*n practical work with persons showing addicted behavior, many characteristics marking the logic of addiction, some of which we shall examine below, stand out strikingly. In our opinion it is necessary to understand these characteristics in order to create a realistic starting point for recovery and/or disentanglement from addiction. This base allows us to take a stable therapeutic position when facing the severely impaired personal autonomy found with addiction. Such a professional therapeutic attitude manifests in the ability to maintain a stable mind, reacting neither with euphoria nor with pessimism to clients' actions and to events, and to stay in close contact with them. It permits the therapist to work with them, engaging directly with the well-known impairments, and to attempt to enhance the remaining autonomy potential and gradually extend it. Drawing from a pool of so many characteristics, we concentrate on (1) the contradictory unit of "the need to decide and the obligation to justify," (2) the falling apart of subjective reasons and objectively restorable motives, and (3) the large gaps among thinking, feeling, and doing.

3.1 The contradictory unit of "the need to decide and the obligation to justify"

Antoine de Saint-Exupéry (1900–1944) has an impressive description of the meeting of the little prince with the tippler in Chapter 12 of his famous book *The Little Prince*:

"What are you doing there?" he said to the tippler .... "I'm drinking," replied the tippler. "Why are you drinking?" asked the little prince. "To forget," replied the tippler. "To forget what?" inquired the little prince, already feeling sorry for him. "To forget that I'm ashamed," the tippler confessed, hanging his head. "Ashamed of what?" insisted the little prince, wanting to help him. "Ashamed of drinking!" concluded the tippler, who then completely locked himself up in silence. And the little prince went away, puzzled.

Two important points are addressed here that determine therapeutic work: past actions (consumption) justify current actions (consumption) justify future actions (consumption). Addicted behavior is characterized by contiguous units of convoluted, contradictory decisions and justifications, and this mode may easily spread to those in contact with addicted persons, such as family members or therapists. There is a constant necessity to make, act on, and justify (at least latently) all decisions (Oevermann, 1997; Hildenbrand, 1995). This process is always embedded in a particular social framework, such that the subjectively experienced freedom to act often encounters objective obstacles that may quickly limit the, at first, infinite potential for freedom (Rogers, quoted in Revenstorf, 1993). Humans move between self-control and loss of control, and must learn to integrate this contradictory unit appropriately, molding it skillfully into daily life. Addicted persons have a distorted experience of this situation; therefore, they often misjudge their actual scope of action and existing autonomy. Where loss of control prevails—for instance with their evident dependency problem, which they cannot shed by means of conscious control—they presume autonomy, but when the possibility of self-determination presents itself (e.g., in arranging one's daily life) they do not take advantage of it but allow their stake in autonomy to diminish. The justifications the tippler gives to the little prince seem congruent to this reasoning: "Being ashamed" is based on "Because I drink!" and vice versa. Both arguments belong to spheres that are not easily controlled. Initially, change is not within sight because any attempt at solving a problem, already seen as an escape, is prevented by further escape (into drugs). In the short term a condition of relaxation or happiness is felt, but in the long term one's potential for independence diminishes more and more. This analysis demonstrates the short but practical definition of addiction made by David Foster Wallace (1998) (Interestingly, this definition comes from a man who was an author and professor of literature, not someone from the social sciences):

> "Something is *malignantly* addictive if (1) it causes real problems for the addict, and (2) it offers itself as a relief from the very problems it causes."

From a practical point of view, this means we need to look again and again, together with the addicted person, at what is real and what is not real. This process of learning to separate reality from illusion and delusion is concretely realized in the steps toward autonomy actually undertaken by addicted persons. Thus, strictly speaking, work on the addiction begins when it is finally about changing past habits and standing on one's own two feet. Then is the time to demonstrate whether previous therapeutic work was successful. Success occurs if, in fact, clients undertake steps based in reality (e.g., applying for a job or training, etc.)—even if at first they fail. Failure is not that important; what is, is continuous effort. It is here that differences between self-reporting based on illusory autonomy and actually completed, "real" actions become apparent.

The second important aspect of the example of the little prince and the tippler is the effectiveness of social interaction. One notices that, confronted with the self-destructive behavior of the tippler, the little prince develops compassion, reacts with emotion, and would like to help. Such a naive reaction—a "wish to help"—is counterproductive with severely addicted persons, precisely because their first priority is to learn to do something according to their own impetus, i.e., to be intrinsically motivated, and to separate themselves from their dependence on other people in day-to-day life. At start again, in order to withdraw support for an attitude of nonactivity and nonengagement in the clients, the fewest possible opportunities for distraction are offered and a certain "boredom" is induced. We expect that they will then be compelled to engage with reality—by determining, for example, how to organize each day in a meaningful fashion. Multifarious possibilities for learning result when clients attempt autonomy and face the possibility of failure—a crucial and essential element in the concept of start again. It is assumed that, only if the possibility of failure actually exists in an action or a plan, a real crisis might develop, and with it a real chance for growth in successfully mastering it. To master a crisis—without falling back into the erroneous habit of consumption in the face of failure—is a major progress for addicted persons. Experiencing and mastering crises positively affects their practical life skills for the long term. Then we can speak about "structural transformation," because something new has been attempted.

The In-depth Systemics intervention model (detailed in section 6.1f.) comes into effect during direct interaction with clients. In fact, the therapists are also working on themselves—on their thinking patterns, on the interaction of mental craving and corporeal sensations, and on their own individual socio-biographic development. In systemic terms, "What is valid for clients, is likewise valid for therapists." Therefore, complementing their clients, the therapists must not withdraw like the little prince when facing refusal. This requires a constant process of self-reflection in order to recognize mutual transference and emotional reactions, and to deal with them with full awareness. Thus it becomes clear that all interventions initiated by therapists are filtered by the subjective constructions of clients. Of course, the same is true in reverse: all the actions of the clients are filtered by the subjective constructions of therapists. If such interventions are seen as rejections, taken personally, or not understood as manifestations of the structure of addicted behavior, then therapy is threatened with failure in the long term because a resilient therapeutic relationship does not develop.

The principle we need to apply is this: ways of behaving may be rejected but not persons. Here awareness, and wisdom built through awareness, enable therapists to observe their own emotional and mental-somatic processes with sufficient distance to avoid getting lost in them, suppressing them, or acting them out. With this attitude they can then engage with addicted behavior. This requires continuous work on their own mental models and autonomy, the development of compassion without getting ensnarled in sympathy, the realistic development of an optimism that is not easily shaken, and a methodically controlled contact with clients. This last, depending on the case, calls for the creation of appropriate contexts for reality checks. The underlying process of liberation from thinking patterns, as well as from mental-somatic models, is guided by the practice of Vipassanā meditation. This will be explained in more detail in section 4.3.

3.1.1 Falling apart of subjective justifications and objectively restorable motives

There may be many reasons for an initial motivation for addiction therapy, and the desire for a completely abstinent life is not always preeminent. The following sentence from an application letter[5] to start again stands "quasi-prototypically" for an abundance of motives at the beginning of addiction therapy:

"I want to get a grip on my addiction."

We worked out, on the basis of an analysis using the Objective Hermeneutics method (Oevermann et al., 1979; Oevermann, 2000), that this statement is not identical with the colloquial, "I wish to be free from addiction." This implies the intention never again to come in contact with addiction. In the former, a desire is expressed to control and contain the addiction. Thus it means not to be really free from addiction, because what one holds—what one keeps under control—cannot be released. Unconsciously, a continued but controlled consumption is intended. A past practice in one's life thereby conceptualizes the vision for a future practice. This is not something new; rather, it demonstrates an unconscious effort to maintain the (harmful) status quo. For the addict, the central question then becomes, "how can therapy help me learn to consume drugs safely, without negative physical, personal, and social consequences?" The unavoidable problems this will create in future addiction therapy are obvious. It will be necessary again and again, together with clients, to take up and reflect on their own perspectives, followed by interactions described in section 3.1. Therapists are asked to identify their counterpart's offers of interaction in the context of the case history and to respond appropriately. It becomes clear how much continuous work this means for therapists themselves, forced as they are to overcome their own mental somatic models and worldviews—a very difficult task!

3.2 The large gap among feeling, thinking, and doing

The phenomenon that feeling, thinking, and doing stand incongruently side by side can be observed, for example, when addicted persons reason very seriously about their motives for exiting from addiction or when they envision plans for the future—and yet the next moment, for whatever reasons, consumption is again in the foreground and there is clear risk of an incident. From both the viewpoint of neurobiology (Robinson & Berridge, 2003) and the wisdom of Theravā da Buddhism, addicted actions are processes operating unconsciously. Acting (procurement and consumption) is initiated and steered from a deep level that is not accessible to most people. How the action is guided is also beyond awareness. At the time addicted persons experience the push of maximum desire for drugs (craving, or in their language, "the itch"), we observe that they are still able to give information about themselves and their internal processes of desire in a strangely dissociated, indifferent way. However, this observation needs to be evaluated independently of their ability to be aware of drug craving as such, to detach from it gradually, and to counter the insatiable thirst with something. Here we see that intellectual understanding has no effective influence on actual action. The major task of in-depth treatment of addiction must therefore be to impart to addicted persons experiences that enable them to make an analytical study of the phenomenon of their own addiction within their own mind-body system. Awareness and wisdom, or, as practiced at start again, Ānāpāna-sati and Vipassanā, are the tools of choice to experience addiction on the mental-somatic level and dissolve it gradually. The direct experience of one's own addiction on this level leads simultaneously to its slow dissolution. It means that one experiences directly *what addiction actually is* through intensive engagement with oneself in oneself. This experience leads to the development of a personal wisdom, i.e., how one has to work personally with one's own mental-somatic addiction complex in order to allow self-healing processes to occur.

The central point of the experience is that the addiction arises, pushes for consumption, and then subsides. If the tendency for consumption is not supported by a reaction of craving, but instead is observed with awareness of the corporeal sensations, it disappears.

In order to better understand this complex mechanism, the theoretical principles of addiction as they are relevant to start againare presented below. In this connection the integration of sociological, psychological, and neurobiological theories, as well as the enduring wisdom of the historical Buddha, appears not only possible, but is indeed necessary.

Notes

5. This application letter is analyzed in much more detail in Studer (1995).

4

The theory is that dopamine-enhancing chemicals fool the brain into thinking drugs are as beneficial as nectar to the bee, thus hijacking a natural reward system that dates back millions of years.

Addicted, TIME, May 5, 1997
J. Madeleine Nash

Models to explain addiction

There is an abundance of theories about the genesis and maintenance of addiction.[6] We have selected those that have been influential in guiding and shaping the therapeutic concept at start again. Important are: (1) a sociological background that was originally inspired by Objective Hermeneutics and the Meilen school of system therapeutics, (2) the neurobiological considerations as originally worked out by Robinson & Berridge (1993), and (3) the practically aligned instructional system of the Theravā da, the teaching of the historical Buddha, Siddhattha Gotama, as it has come down to us.

4.1 The sociological background

Initially, the work at start again was shaped by the methodology of the Objective Hermeneutics (reconstruction of meaning) of Ulrich Oevermann (2000) and the Meilen school of system therapeutics (Welter-Enderlin & Hildenbrand, 1996). Objective Hermeneutics offers a methodical framework to access cases through their inherent logic. At the center is general human behavior or activity, which in a certain social and historical context constitutes an individual's life. In each individual case the structure of action and perception is worked out in the sense of a methodological controlled diagnosis, and this is used to guide and adapt therapeutic action individually. Sociological experience is considered within the well-known structures of society, family, and the individual. The system-therapeutic basics influence concrete (everyday life) therapeutic work and the mode of interaction with clients.

The sequence analysis method (Hildenbrand, 1996, 2005b) allows analysis of any form of text (discussion minutes, interactions, genograms; see Hildenbrand, 2005a) in terms of their structures of meaning. It permits the examination of life ambitions, progression of addiction, or whole family biographies in such a way that important topics and problematic complexes can be identified, as well as important resources and support for clients (Stachowske, 2002, for a multigenerational perspective on addiction). Structural principles of each case can thus be derived (Hildenbrand, 1996), leading to the identification of various types (Hildenbrand, 2005b; Kluge, 2000).

Realizations gained in the process are introduced into therapy and permit an individually adapted procedure. Sequence analysis works strictly logically according to a succession of formulating and testing of hypotheses by means of the falsification criterion as set out by Popper (1943). Texts, i.e., the natural genesis of language that is the objectively observable gestalt expressing a way of life, are sequentially examined and analyzed in their natural succession as they build one on the other. For additional literature we refer the reader to the volumes of Hildenbrand (2005b, 2005a) and Wernet (2000).

The structure-oriented view of socialization (Oevermann, 1997) gives, in addition, a model that describes how a way of life develops over the course of years, which tasks of development are to be mastered, and/or what kind of damage can develop. Socialization can be understood as a succession of displacement crises, and a particular way of life always occurs between diffuse and specific social relations.

Diffuse (or person-oriented) social relationships are those between individuals, which are found prototypically in the primary family (parents' relationship, parent-child relationships). Their characteristic (Oevermann, 1996) is that thematically anything can be introduced and that the people involved are not exchangeable. Specific (or role-oriented) social relationships are precisely characterized by the restriction of the spectrum of what can be brought up as an issue. Issues raised have to be justified, and the roles remain constant even if people (e.g., therapists) change. These two concepts can easily be distinguished by stating that diffuse social relationships are private relationships within one's family, whereas specific social relationships are those that happen in social interaction with the public, in professional contexts, etc. Addicts generally fail to differentiate between these two concepts, or at least in those cases where their routines and habits fail: when they should act one way, they act the other, and vice versa. This leads to serious problems in their daily life. One reason is that diffuse social relationships always turn into specific social relationships when they fail, and then the basic forms of sociability cease to function.

The oedipal triad is a special case of such a displacement crisis. In this context it does not correspond to the development of the classic Oedipus complex as described by Sigmund Freud, but is "borrowed" from him (Oevermann, 1996). At the time of development of the oedipal constellation (at about age 4 or 5), one experiences that the exclusive claim on a partner in a diffuse social relationship must be shared with a third person. The experiences of social inclusion and exclusion, arising mostly with the parents, have to be integrated. They form the basis for a deep positive experience of a nonresolvable contradictory unit. If this developmental phase is not experienced properly and integrated successfully, harmful seeds are planted that grow and manifest in future social settings. These seeds frequently contribute to the deep roots of addiction, which can therefore be understood as a search for alleged clarity when facing nonresolvable contradictions. To master the emerging dynamics requires the individual to learn to reconcile the alternating phases of social inclusion and exclusion and to shape them as part of life. The basic task is not to solve nonresolvable contradictions, but to accept them and learn to establish distance from them so that their influence is minimized. If this integration succeeds, it is accepted that a person is equipped with a good basis for mastering subsequent life crises. However, in the case of addicted persons we often find pathogenic constellations in this area (early mother and/or father-child relationships). start again is guided by the concept of "therapy in daily life and daily life as therapy" (Hildenbrand, 1991). The application of this concept helps clients in a multitude of settings to differentiate naturally between diffuse and specific social relationships. In doing so, deeply rooted patterns come to light that initially settle mostly into more of the same instead of becoming part of transformative solutions to problematic social interaction or inability to accomplish practical daily tasks. However, it is at this stage that beneficial therapeutic interactions and encounters emerge. Basically, for the addict, the therapeutic aim is to learn to treat the crisis as the norm, and to align oneself with constantly changing environmental conditions and one's own desires and needs without gliding into drug consumption for short-term relief. In using the term "crisis," we refer here to the assumption that, if routines and habits fail, a crisis results .

A central realization of work with addicted persons is that a resocialization, in the sense of recovering lost abilities and authority, is mostly not what comes to the fore. Rather, socialization must be supplemented and enhanced in order to train underdeveloped competencies or strengthen them in such a way that clients can lead as autonomous a life as possible (e.g. look for a place to live, a job, etc.) without floundering from crisis to crisis and finally to the edge of a serious incident. Therefore we speak instead of "*post*-socialization." The autobiographical work done by the clients (family history, addiction career) that they present in front of their peers represents a significant component of the therapy program because of the importance of this post-socialization. The connection between therapy and everyday life is also supported by an arrangement whereby clients live together in a protected environment in housing groups of three to four persons and so have an immediate space in which they have to face each other.

Life can be summarized as an interplay of self-control and a lack thereof, crisis and routine, as well as the need to decide and the obligation to vindicate. Promotion of the ability to bear and integrate these contradictory units, or actively to shape them, is the major task of the therapy. A life-practical attitude of "as-well-as" is to be developed contrary to the predominating "either-or" of addicted thinking and doing.

4.2 The neurobiological basis

Current neurobiological explanation models for the genesis and maintenance of addiction go back to the groundbreaking article by Robinson & Berridge (1993) with its "hypothesis of incentive (salience) learning." This quasi-paradigmatic article reasons on the basis of empirical studies that the classical learning theories (positive reinforcement, negative reinforcement) cannot explain satisfactorily the genesis nor the continued consumption found in addiction. Instead, its authors establish a neurobiologically justified model in which the emotional evaluation processes of sensory stimuli take a central role. In what follows, we refer to the original position taken by Robinson and Berridge. Although the authors have published many more articles on the topic, their initial position still seems to be valid and empirically well-founded. Their 1993 article is extraordinary, summarizing the main points of their discussion in a very simple and elegant way. Interested readers who want to investigate the neurobiological basis of addiction might care to refer to the comprehensive book by Koob & LeMoal (2006), as well as the more recent articles by Robinson and Berridge (1995, 2000, 2001, 2003, 2004, 2008, 2009), Robinson et al. (2005), Berridge et al. (2009), Berridge (2007), Berridge & Kringelbach (2008), Berridge et al. (1984, 2009), Peciña et al. (2006), Smith & Berridge (2007), Winkielman & Berridge (2003), and Wyvell & Berridge (2000). The websites of both Kent C. Berridge[7] and Terry E. Robinson[8] provide direct and free access to reprints of their articles. A deeper understanding of the position of the incentive (salience) hypothesis emerges if the reader is also familiar with common concepts of motivation and action psychology (e.g., see Heckhausen, 1989).

4.2.1 A critique of the classical learning theories

According to Robinson & Berridge (1993, 2003), there is sufficient empirical evidence suggesting that drugs are not taken in order to *escape distress* because:

- Drugs are not taken exclusively due to unpleasant conditions.
- Withdrawal distress is not correlated with periods of maximal drug self-administration, e.g., because motivation is low at times of maximum withdrawal pain and only afterwards again rises slowly.
- Renewed drug consumption can suddenly and unexpectedly begin (e.g., triggered by crises), even after years of abstinence during which withdrawal symptoms have not been felt for a long time.
- Freedom from the agony of withdrawal has little to do with continued drug consumption.
- Maximum reported craving is often observed directly after drug consumption and not when facing withdrawal pain.
- Substances that cause withdrawal symptoms when used purely medically do not necessarily produce craving.

Furthermore, one should contrast the thesis that drugs are taken to *seek pleasure* with the following:

- Initial drug consumption is often not actually pleasant; however, it can from the beginning produce massive craving since addictive substances can cause persistent neural changes from first exposure.
- Continued consumption leads to a substantial loss of social and physical well-being (crime, prostitution, disease, malnutrition,

social isolation, loss of work, partners, and friends). However, in general this does not deter drug use.

- Subjectively addicted persons are often irritated at themselves and their own actions, i.e., they use drugs without really feeling a hedonistic pleasure from the consumption.

Thus it can be stated that *liking* drugs is separate from *wanting* and *using* drugs. This suggests that two different cycles are operating. In their "hypothesis of incentive learning," Robinson and Berridge describe a process of genesis and maintenance of addiction with four characteristics:

- All addictive drugs share the potential to initiate long-term neural adjustments in the brain. They ensure that, even on a neural level, consumption continues.
- Change occurs to those areas of the brain that are brought into a causal connection with motivation and reward, particularly the nucleus accumbens (NA), the ventral tegmentum area (VTA) with dopamine as transmitting substance, and the various projections of the mesolimbic area which reach to the prefrontal cortex (PFC).
- Addictive drugs hypersensitize these brain areas. This means that continued consumption leads to states in which neural responses run ever faster and more easily, thus representing the inverse of tolerance formation.
- The sensitized brain areas do not convey hedonistic or euphoric effects, but incentive salience—"significance." In the course of sensitization, a learning process is activated that charges the recognized (situational, social, geographical, financial, etc.) impulses with a hint or suggestion that successful drug consumption is of vital significance. Later these hinting impulses work as triggers for the operant seeking and taking of drugs.

Nash (1997) states that incentive learning always happens when *there is a better reward than expected*. This quickly forms a habit so that greed for an ever higher reward becomes independent of the original context. From this complex succession of (emotional) evaluation and learning processes it follows after Nash (ibid., p.49) that:

"[a]ddicts do not crave heroin or cocaine or alcohol or nicotine per se, but want the rush of dopamine that these drugs produce."

If the approach by Robinson and Berridge is connected with the "hypothesis of somatic markers" (Damasio, 1994), then the gap initially described among feeling, thinking, and doing is more comprehensible. The "hypothesis of somatic markers" (ibid.) sketches a model for human decision making and actions, as well as one of consciousness (Damasio, 1999), which accords an integral role to corporeal sensations and superimposed emotional evaluations. It is important to understand the contribution of these sensations to the special forms of thinking, feeling, deciding, and doing by addicted persons. If this interaction between corporeal sensations and emotional evaluations is strongly disturbed, then the intellectual processes cannot build on it and introduce changes.

Addiction therapy thus requires direct experience of one's addiction based on corporeal sensations, in such a way that one works directly with them as the mental objects of addiction. The section on Theravā da and Vipassanā describes how and why this can succeed. "How addiction feels" must be experienced, and so too that addiction is not directed toward the substances per se but toward the type of sensation felt which is triggered by them and/or the recollection of them.

In the course of research following on from the work of Robinson and Berridge, modifications have been suggested by Di Chiara (1995b, 1995a), Volkow et al. (1999), and others, but the fundamental mechanism of incentive learning has not so far been refuted—either on a theoretical or empirical level (Robinson & Berridge (2008); Robinson et al. (2005); Berridge (2005, 2007)). This approach is still deemed to have great significance and explanatory power.

There are, however, some limitations to these neurobiological explanations. One is the super-elevated functioning attributed to the brain which is awarded characteristics that should actually be attributed to the whole person (Bennett & Hacker, 2003). This is seen in the formulation of the "addicted brain," which is to be found in nearly every recent specialized scientific article on the neurobiology of addiction. Such a one-sided view neglects other areas of possible significance, like the enteric nervous system (Gershon, 2001) or cell-memory, with their potential but still unexplored influence on addiction-memory and addicted acting. We would be well advised, therefore, to be aware—as clearly enunciated in Wittgenstein's (1921/1963) philosophy of language—of the immense influence that linguistic construction can have on interpretation and on the subsequent direction of research.

These cited limitations of neurobiology that—from our point of view—are often neglected, have an enormous influence on actual therapeutic practice. If, for example, therapists think only of an "addicted brain" when they work with clients, then they might not recognize a client's potential to overcome certain difficulties (believing an "addicted brain" is not capable of this or that). Such a fixed world view is also present in some types of self-help groups, e.g., the "anonymous" groups which assume that addiction is always a life-long condition, like an incurable disease. Thus, we should take great care in developing our own mental-somatic models. Although there is no doubt that drugs seriously damage the brain and might do so for a very long time, even permanently, an addict is more than just a brain. Like everyone else, addicts can change their lifestyle and, not only recover from addiction, have the potential to be completely free from drugs and addiction. It must be kept in mind that addicts can fail and *start again*—like everyone else. Unfortunately, neurobiology can be misinterpreted resulting in low-lying potentials being overlooked in therapeutic work. We should investigate neurobiological findings with great interest, because we can learn a great deal from them—e.g., limits due to the physical consequences of long-term drug consumption. We should be aware, however, that neurobiology is just one of many disciplines that explore the phenomenon of addiction.

4.3 The contributions of the Theravāda to the In-depth Systemics approach towards addiction

The age-old wisdom of Theravāda Buddhism is accepted in its key statements as the historically accurate transmission of the teaching of the Buddha (Schumann, 1999, 2000, 2001). Although the written record of the Pāli canon, or Tipiṭaka (see U Ko Lay, 1995, for a summary of its content), is extensive, the teaching itself can be summed up by these few words in verse 183 of the Dhammā pada (Buddhist Publication Society, 1985), translated from the Pāli by Buddharakkhita Thera:

"To avoid all evil, to cultivate good, and to cleanse one's mind—this is the teaching of the Buddhas."

A major element in the practical teaching of the Buddha is the Four Noble Truths (ariya sacca, Goenka, 1991, 1997): (1) the truth of suffering, (2) the truth of the cause of suffering, (3) the truth of the extinction of suffering, and (4) the truth of the way to extinguish suffering, known as the Noble Eightfold Path (ariyo aṭṭhaṅgiko maggo). Suffering is equated to attachment to and craving (taṇhā) for the objects of the six sensory organs (the five corporeal sense organs plus the mind). The Buddha's signal contribution was his discovery, through direct experience and analysis of the mind-body system and mental structures, that corporeal sensations (vedanā), caused by contact between the six sense organs and their respective objects, are a direct and tangible link between mind and body (Goenka, 1998). In the Pāḷi canon this is expressed as:

"vedanā-samosaranā sabbe dhamma" (Aṅguttara Nikāya, V.R.I., 2000, III Dasakanipāta 58)[9],

translated in V.R.I. (ibid.) as: "Everything that arises in the mind flows together with sensations." Whatever arises in the mind (e.g., a memory, a thought, an emotion) is accompanied by a corporeal sensation. Suffering develops if one reacts to these sensations by wanting them (craving, clinging), or wanting them to go away (aversion, hatred). Reality is not then recognized as it actually is, according to its true characteristics: changing (anicca), suffering (dukkha), and without any essence other than cause-and-effect relationships (anattā). Attempting to cling to something that continuously changes creates suffering. Consequently, insight into these characteristics realized through direct experience, based on direct experience (bhāvāna-mayā paññā), removed from blind faith or intellectual acrobatics, leads to the extinguishing of suffering (V.R.I., 1993). But to be successful, to appreciate reality as it is, one must observe the changes in the corporeal sensations with awareness and without reaction. In this way sensations serve as a tool for the mind to observe its own workings. Mental attachments are dissolved automatically providing the mind does not cling to them. The direct realization of change broadens into the realization of suffering and of nonessence. Wisdom (paññā) develops if the practice is carried out with an ethical attitude (sīla), with a concentrated mind (samādhi), and with continuity.

Sīla, samādhi and paññā are the three quintessential practices of the Noble Eightfold Path (Goenka, 1991, 1997, 1998). For laypeople, sīla is the abstention from killing, lying, stealing, sexual misconduct, and any consumption of alcohol or other intoxicating substances (i.e., drugs). The actions that one avoids oneself are also not to be endorsed or encouraged in others. One not only abstains from unwholesome actions, one also performs wholesome actions, helpful to others.

Samādhi is the ability to keep the mind continuously concentrated on one point. To develop this ability, one practices the technique of Ānāpāna-sati (Mājjhima Nikāya, V.R.I., 2000, III 149), the observation of the breath as it naturally comes in and goes out of the nostrils. According to the Buddha, as a preliminary stage to Vipassanā, concentration must be developed with the help of an object constantly present and free from attachments. The normal inflow and outflow of the breath is ideal for this purpose.

Paññā is the wisdom one acquires through the practice. This wisdom is realized through direct experience, because only by direct experience—i.e., through "living wisdom"—do actual changes in life occur. The Buddha distinguished three types of paññā:

- Sutta-mayā paññā—wisdom acquired through learning (i.e., hearing it from others)
- Cintā-mayā paññā—wisdom based on intellectual reasoning (i.e., by ratiocination or reasoning)
- Bhāvanā-mayā paññā —wisdom as a consequence of direct experience (within the framework of the body).

Paññā that arises from the proper practice of Vipassanā is the wisdom by which a practitioner understands the structure of the body and the mind, and their interaction at the deepest level. As a consequence, a s/he no longer reacts in ignorance, but is capable of conscious and thoughtful actions guided by positive intentions, good for oneself and good for others.

The technique of Vipassanā is practiced as the equanimous observation of one's mind-body system, conveyed through the corporeal sensations that are the object of meditation. Vipassanā is described in detail in the Pāli canon in the Mahāsatipaṭṭhāna Suttaṃ (V.R.I., 1993).

The technique, in essence, is the perfect establishment of awareness [10] (in four variants: on the body, on the sensations, on the mind, and on the mind's contents)—ātāpi sampajāno satimā[11] (ibid.)—the continuous concentrated observation of corporeal sensations with wisdom (paññā), i.e., with an appreciation of their changing, afflictive, and essenceless (non-self) nature.

The translation of Satipaṭṭhāna as "establishing awareness" combines the sense of developing and applying, implying that this is not a unique act but a process progressing toward increased awareness and wisdom.

It is thus a continuous practicing of awareness and wisdom. The Buddha emphasizes the practice of the Noble Eightfold Path with Vipassanā (the term is to be understood as identical to Satipaṭṭhāna, Goenka, 1998) as the principal and universal means for the complete removal of suffering and/or mental impurities. The In-depth Systemics approach in its engagement with addiction uses this universality of the practice: addicted persons react with attachment to their own corporeal sensations, which are triggered by consuming substances and/or through impulses learned along with consumption. From this point of view, the Buddha's approach appears to be virtually tailored for dealing with addiction—taking into account that, for success, it must be practiced correctly and continuously. The exit from addiction leads through the acceptance and recognition of the nature of one's own corporeal sensations. In this way wisdom (paññā) develops regarding oneself which is, perhaps, of an intellectual nature or founded on blind faith, but nonetheless arises from one's own direct experience within one's own mind-body system.

For most addicts, initially, the practice of Vipassanā is inordinately challenging. They are often confused and their mental state very unstable. For the technique to work for them, they at first need to calm their minds down to gain some degree of stability and quietude. This is achieved through a regular and prolonged practice of awareness of breath (Ānāpāna-sati). After several months of continuous practice of (Ānāpāna-sati), they are prepared to learn Vipassanā. Their principal task is to understand that their addictions are rooted in ignorant reactions to their own corporeal sensations. Through observation of bodily sensations they come to understand, step by step, that it is not the drugs they have consumed that is their main problem; rather, the craving for these drugs is more important, and this craving has become the burdensome pattern of their minds. As S.N. Goenka states in his evening discourses during a tenday Vipassanā meditation course, at first people crave for drugs, alcohol, etc., but in the long run they just crave for the feeling of craving. All the harmful activities and consequences (drug-seeking behavior, drug consumption, loss of social and physical wellbeing, etc.) are related to that craving pattern.

The contradictory units that were cited above (in section 3.1) can be integrated by observing these corporeal sensations with equanimity. Whether individuals can maintain mental stability and thus experience wisdom and happiness, or whether, by endless loops of reactions of attachment (aversion, craving), they increase their suffering, is seen in their practice. In the latter case, the closely circumscribed addiction has transformed into a fundamental habitual attitude of addiction—meaning specifically, attachment to and craving for the pleas ant qualities, or rejection of the unpleasant qualities, of the ever changing corporeal sensations. In this context their impermanence creates suffering because attachment to something that is constantly changing—according to the Theravāda view of mind-body—can only create suffering.

Through the practice of Vipassanā one can learn to experience this impermanence directly, facing it without losing one's peace of mind. Therefore practicing Vipassanā is at the core of In-depth Systemics (see section 6.1ff.). Every moment in which the reality of the constantly changing mind-body system is experienced at the level of bodily sensations is a treatment for the addiction at a very deep level. Consequently, no fundamental difference exists between substance-bound and substance-free addictions. Addiction can be to anything. Likewise the "remedy" is universally applicable. Through training in the equanimous observation of corporeal sensations, a lasting treatment for addiction is available that is independent of the outwardly observable quality of the addiction.

However, it would be unwarranted to conclude that an isolated "administration" of Vipassanā as a one-off intervention will quickly "heal" an addiction. In therapeutic practice one soon learns that existing forms of damaged autonomy, i.e., missing life skills competencies, insufficient interactive behavior, an incomplete education, etc., require a multi-modal program. Nevertheless, actual in-depth work on addiction can be equated with continuous practice of Vipassanā , since the deep-rooted mental reaction patterns can thereby be reached and gradually dissolved. With addiction, however, this only succeeds within an integrated, psychotherapeutic, social, rehabilitation frame-work.

Notes

6. An overview of various models to explain addiction can be found in Scholz (1992)

7. www.lsa.umich.edu/psych/research&labs/berridge/publications.htm

8. http://sitemaker.umich.edu/terryrobinson/publications

9. see also V.R.I. 1993, footnote 3

10. A precise investigation of the challenging task of adequately translating the terms "Satipaṭṭhāna" and "Vipassanā " (especially in the context

of the Mahāsatipaṭṭhāna Suttaṃ) was done elsewhere (Scholz, 1992, chapter 9.1). In that work, the author also discussed and compared the various interpretations of Satipaṭṭhāna and Vipassanā. Goenka (V.R.I., 1993) translates the term Satipaṭṭhāna as "the establishing of awareness."

11. The right understanding of mindfulness and wisdom can be identified by the usage of the term "sampajañña" which is a very important and fundamental term in the Pāḷi canon. In his discourses, S.N. Goenka translates the term as "constant thorough understanding of impermanence."

Chapter

5

The competence for autonomy requires the experience of
emotional bonding, attachment, and happiness.

*Offenders: How Ordinary People Become
Mass Murderers*
HARALD WELZER

Consequences — the goal of therapeutic actions in addiction therapy

After the theoretical explanations of addiction above, a lofty ideal of therapeutic action can be formulated:

The ideal of therapeutic action is (re)establishing an autonomous life through an in-depth engagement with the addiction.

5.1 What in practical terms is needed for recovery from addiction?

In practical terms, for recovery from addiction a solution is needed for the difficulties that many clients face when starting to address their situation. Besides their addiction, they are often burdened with experiences of failed diffuse social relationships, have little competence in day-to-day life skills, are traumatized, and—increasingly in recent years—experience co-morbidities, and personality and affective disorders (Axis II disorders, DSM-IV[12]). As already discussed, addicted persons exhibit inappropriate ways of dealing with social reality. There is no balance between self-interest and an orientation toward the common good. The shaping of past and future out of the here and now hardly exists, and acceptance of the perspectives of others and the demarcation of "I" versus others only succeeds with difficulty.[13] Their problems are amplified by their projections and illusionary subjective feeling of autonomy that objectively emerges mostly as illusory autonomy, where feelings of little self-worth and shame are concealed behind vaunted importance. With this background, addicted persons repeatedly "cross the line" during their daily therapeutic life at start again. Due to their lifestyle of searching for drugs and drug procurement, they are masters at deceiving, cheating, and disguising.[14]

Under these circumstances, a lot of patience and frustration tolerance is required on the part of the therapists in finding and establishing workable personal relationships with the clients.

However, one should not confound this initial situation with pathogenic constellations. Every addicted person also brings his or her individually specific resources, which together we have to identify and access (through sociological methods such as work with genograms, etc.; see section 4.1) in order to activate an increase in autonomy. Life skills formed by socialization are not consistent. Nonetheless, it is important to know what the current reality is, what (for the time being) has aspirational character, and what (at least for now) is perhaps simply impossible. Therefore, there is no general answer to the question of how to motivate a client. Rather, in each individual case we must try to meet the person where s/he is now, offer suitable learning contexts, and consistently demand developmental steps that can be reconstructed and are appropriate to that individual.

In daily therapeutic life we must repeatedly provide tailored contexts for reality checks. Here a mixture of demands, e.g., to show participation and post-socialization in order to work on specific inadequacies, is required. Learning from success, from the experience that one can achieve of one's own accord, is held to be an important factor at start again. All of this reflects once more the logic of "therapy in daily life and daily life as therapy."

Lasting success is recognized when clients are compelled to stand on their own two feet. The protective shell of the in-house situation becomes thinner, and clients merge more acutely with the reality of everyday life. What was really learned in the protected in-house setting and what is transferable outside will now be seen. We cannot always read correctly from the course the therapy has taken whether someone will later lead a successful drug-free life. Therefore, incidents (i.e., renewed drug consumption) are not a criterion for failure, but a cause to reflect together on what can be learned, what the trigger was, and how to find a new approach to facing crises in future. Only too often do we observe that apparently difficult clients show a subsequently successful recovery, while "model" clients encounter substantial problems a short time after leaving therapy. It is precisely the many crises, and the experience of mastering them, that builds for the former clients the necessary practical life competencies. These may have been missed by those who passed through the therapy "successfully," and who were rarely forced, or had no opportunity, to face their problems, and were therefore not compelled to do the transformative work within themselves. We call this the "principle of failure": i.e., for real success there must be a potential for failure during the therapeutic process and also afterwards. If one can fail, one can learn. This is an inductive principle that is also applied in totally different contexts. For example, Edwin T. Jaynes, a well-known physicist, states in his 2003 book:

> "If the predictions prove to be wrong, then induction has served its real purpose."

Wisdom concerning failure is reflected in the life principle, "Who dares wins." The possible failure of one's life vision emerges here as the potential in, "Nothing ventured, nothing gained."

In summary, the "ideal" intervention process that was mentioned at the beginning of this section regarding the specific basic conditions for the recovery from addiction can best be summarized by saying that it is always about devising a well-founded and methodologically controlled procedure for each individual case—i.e., adaptive therapy.

Notes

12. The Diagnostic and Statistical Manual of Mental Disorders (DSM) is published by the American Psychiatric Association.

13. An elaborate reconstruction of the specific type of damaged autonomy in addiction can be found in Studer (1998, chapter 3).

14. In German, summarized as the "three Ts": Tricksen, Täuschen und Tarnen. This alliterative word-play does not quite work in English translation.

Here is my secret. It is very simple: It is only with the heart
that one can see rightly; what is essential is
invisible to the eye.

The Little Prince
Antoine de Saint-Exupéry

Intervention and the In-depth Systemics approach

6.1 The concept of start again

Start again is an In-depth Systemics-oriented institution to help people be free of addiction (from drugs, etc.). As such, it is envisioned as an abstinence and exit-oriented institution compatible with the teaching of the Theravāda described above. Just as an in-depth engagement with addiction is not possible if the mind is in contact with addictive substances, so too abstaining from mind-altering substances is an integral part of sīla and the Noble Eightfold Path. Without sīla the mind is not able to explore deeper realities and therefore cannot develop wisdom from direct experience.

The entire program, which can take up to 18 months, and in exceptional cases even longer, is divided into two parts: an in-house component with intensive therapeutic attendance (including biographical work), and a reintegration component that focuses on professional and social rehabilitation. This concept permits flexible adjustment to individual clients as well as the use of personnel and resources adequate to a particular situation. Since, as described above, addiction manifests precisely when responsibility must be assumed, for an in-depth engagement with one's own addiction great importance is given to the reintegration component.

The vision for the future is a complete client-driven program without any distinction between the in-house and social reintegration components. Such an approach has however to be prepared carefully.

Some of these considerations have already been discussed in greater detail by Studer (1998).

On the practical side, at start again we ensure that physical and social elements are promoted appropriately, including a balanced vegetarian diet, sports (Iyengar yoga, among other things), and rehabilitation of any seriously compromised body parts (e.g., the teeth in particular). All this is limited by the dictum not to offer too much to clients so as not to support their ingrained "consumer" attitude, since this would undermine the overall concept.

For analytic purposes, the In-depth Systemics therapy concept of start again is subdivided into four pillars that together constitute the foundation and essence of the approach:

1. systemic addiction therapy,
2. systemic family therapy,
3. self-help (NA[15] and RRS[16]), and
4. meditation techniques (Ānāpāna-sati and Vipassanā).

Due to experiences within various fields of practice, the In-depth Systemics approach has currently been enhanced (see section 6.5). The systemic aspects of therapy are, as previously mentioned, along the lines of the Meilen school. In addition to the concept of "everyday life as therapy and therapy as everyday life," additional essential dynamics of living and learning together have been created. Self-help groups facilitate the beneficial role of peer coaching and post-socialization. They also play an important role because addicted persons, like almost everyone else, learn a great deal from their peers. Addicts clearly understand the tactics of other addicts. For peer coaches, this interaction unfortunately often reactivates their own mental-somatic models of addiction, and they have to be careful to keep a personal distance. Professionals (therapists, social workers, etc.) can better distance themselves from addicts; their main problem is to see through the addicts' various tactics and games (see Scholz, 1992 for a critical discussion of the organizations AA and NA).

Ānāpāna-sati and Vipassanā are the techniques employed to engage addiction at its deepest level and gradually dissolve it by facing it. In accordance with the logic of the Theravāda, the practice of Ānāpāna-sati leads to a calming of the mind, while Vipassanā "cleanses" the mind by the experience of anicca, i.e., impermanence (Goenka, 1991, 1998). This experience of impermanence at the level of the corporeal sensations (vedanā) leads, ideally, to observing within oneself the arising and passing away of craving without reacting to the simultaneously felt sensations; instead, one follows their arising and passing with a balanced mind. This is, however, an ambitious goal that clients can approximate only gradually and in part. Nevertheless, as a goal, it exerts a powerful influence.

Ānāpāna-sati is taught at start again as part of a mandatory program (twice daily, in the morning and in the evening, each session between 30 and 60 minutes). In addition, one day each month is wholly dedicated to the practice of Ānāpāna-sati. Addicts learn to observe not only breath but also the arising and passing away of sensations at the entrance to the nostrils, which helps to develop paññā (wisdom regarding the changing nature of mind and matter), as was discussed in section 4.3. This is requisite preparation for a future ten-day Vipassanā course, during which the shift in focus from pure breath to sensations is taught on day three. Therefore the Ānāpāna- sati day provides a link between awareness of breath and the actual technique of Vipassanā: that is, observation of sensations with equanimity.

To learn the Vipassanā technique, clients attend ten-day courses at an external Vipassanā center. Courses[17] are conducted in the tradition of the prominent Burmese meditation teacher Sayagyi U Ba Khin, as taught by Mr. S.N. Goenka. Attending a Vipassanā course is, as a matter of principle, a voluntary decision. Clients may apply after adequate stabilization and sufficient practice of Ānāpāna-sati. Personnel also have an opportunity to learn and practice the meditation technique, an aspect of In-depth Systemics explicitly promoted by start again. In fact, the quality of work in an In-depth Systemics institution (whether with addicts or not) depends on the actual practice of the people working there. If the therapists, social workers, etc., do not attempt to dissolve their own mental-somatic models by applying self-observation at the level of sensations (regardless of what this process is called), they cannot really expect clients to do so with maximum effort. In addition, as long as the professionals do not practice awareness and wisdom meditation, they can never really understand the experiences and processes of the clients who do. They will lack the capability to penetrate the deeper aspects of mind and body and will never fully understand what addiction is nor how to overcome it. How will they then be able to help clients in a professional way? So far as In-depth Systemics is concerned, self-practice is essential.

6.2 Short outline of In-depth Systemics

The In-depth Systemics view of human nature is outlined in Studer (1998). Historically, the first statements on In-depth Systemics and the basic concept go back to the founder of start again, Gerhard Scholz, and the therapeutic leader in its early years at the beginning of the 1990s, Sergio Mantovani. Using the practice of Vipassanā as a basis, the concept of In-depth Systemics was shaped by the continuous effort to optimize and refine the clinical social-rehabilitative work of the institution toward the goal of a high level professionalism. The start again evaluation study (Studer, 1998, chapter 7) introduced the approach for the first time along with precise theoretical explanations. The approach was, moreover, translated into neurobiological terms and expressed in relation to the integral role of Vipassanā meditation.

6.3 The initial model and autonomy

The initial model of In-depth Systemics is shown in figure 6.1. Overall, this model integrates the various parts that played a dominant role at that time, with the interdependence of mind and body taking center stage. Vipassanā's role is to allow the work on mental-somatic models. Autonomy also plays a crucial role (see below). The dynamic relationship between individuals and society, as well as neurobiological findings on the physiological aspects of addiction, complete the model.

The core of the model points to the interdependence of mind and body, as well as that of the individual and society. This integration leads to the interleaving of

1. specific damage to personal autonomy in the course of individual biographic processes and socializing developmental processes, and
2. deep-rooted and habitual mental-somatic dynamic reactions at the level of physical sensations where mental desire and bodily sensations are intertwined (craving for pleasant sensations, aversion toward unpleasant ones). Together they produce a harmful dynamic process of mental desire that can never be fully satisfied.

The concept of In-depth Systemics thus arranges social-rehabilitative and psychotherapeutic interventions alongside two processes: (1) the biographic process (both re-socialization and postocialization), and (2) a systematic mental training. Training the

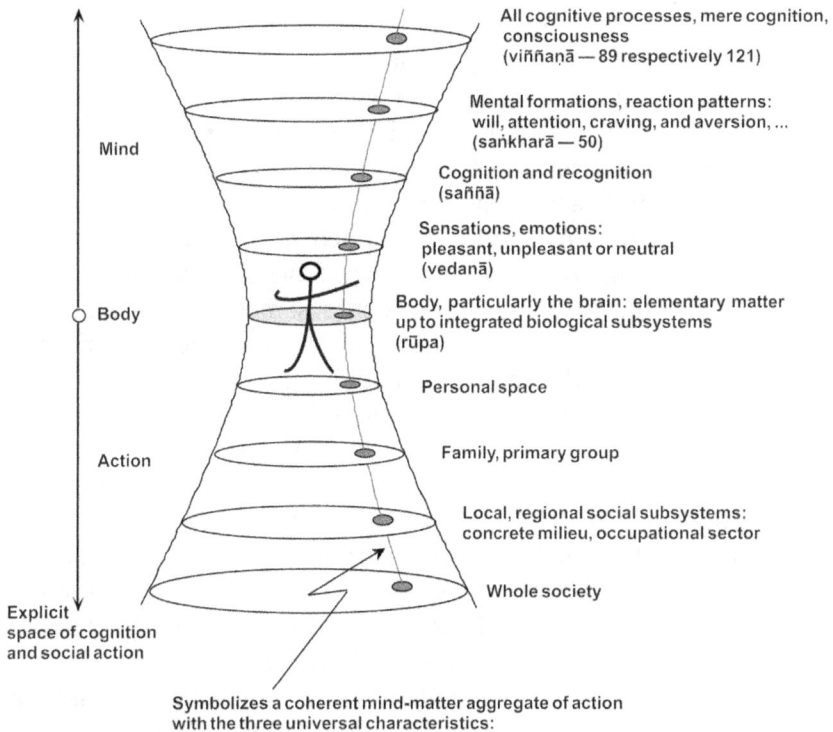

Figure 6.1: *Initial model of the In-depth Systemics approach (Studer, 1998)*

mind is aimed directly at self-realization and its role in dissolving the individual's mental-somatic dynamic of reaction throughout the depths of the mind.

Careful observation reveals the influence of mental-somatic models on all actions that an addict performs in his or her life. Does s/he act out of craving and/or aversion, or is s/he able to handle reality properly in order to make intelligent decisions and act accordingly? This dimension, which we call "autonomy," plays a crucial role in In-depth Systemics, and has two aspects based on the distinction introduced above (individual versus society, and mind versus body), and may therefore be conceptualized in a twofold way:

1. Autonomy encompasses all practical life skills that structure and shape life itself. These take place in the context of the antagonism between the "necessity for decision-making" and the "obligation for justification of decisions," with one's biography in the background. Social situations are ever-

changing and interrelated—the various and endless cause-and-effect relationships that happen throughout a lifetime. Autonomy unfolds, therefore, as the skills required to master them develop in the here-and-now so that navigating incidents and developments in furture will be successful. Shaping one's life means to act wisely so that future events occur as a logical consequence of actions performed at this very moment. It requires one to make something of the current situation, i.e., transform what life presents into something more valuable for a later benefit. In general, life happens between the two endpoints of the spectrum of autonomy: routines and crises. If routines do not work anymore and the usual tactics fail, a crisis ensues. Autonomy can be observed when a person can find new solutions to actual problems, which may entail letting go of ingrained thought patterns, old habits, and familiar routines. Crises, therefore, are opportunities, because they provide all the conditions that serve as a framework for structural transformation. Only in crisis do people really change. The task is to acquire life itself and shape it wisely.

2. Autonomy is also manifest when an individual demonstrates the skills to act free of mental conditionings and blind reaction patterns in such a way that decisions and actions are not based on craving, aversion, or ego. This means that s/he does not blindly follow a desire for bodily sensations. The process that governs whether one acts autonomously or not takes place at the depth of the (unconscious) mind at the level of physical sensations. If a person is able to observe sensations as they are and yet act according to the exigencies of a situation, s/he can be said to be autonomous in decision-making. Autonomy is freedom from desires like craving for pleasant sensations and aversion toward unpleasant ones.

An intervention program should be case-oriented and guided by the specific case itself, including the respective strengths and damages the client brings to it. At the beginning of each therapeutic process it is thus necessary to work out the specific resources, as well as the deficiencies, of the client. This diagnostic process has, of course, to be repeated from time to time to allow structural transformation to take place, or even to be noticed. Capabilities and shortcomings have to be identified in a controlled, methodical way so that no dysfunctional mental projections from therapists or other persons involved shape the reconstruction that underlies the therapeutic strategy for the case.

6.4 Recovery from addiction

Recovery from addiction describes a process in which there is progress in the sense of augmenting resources and reducing deficiencies within the natural boundaries of the case: i.e., an increase in relative autonomy. Progress then corresponds to reality and one expects it to be reliable and stable. The therapeutic ideal is assistance with self-help, whereby the degree of therapeutic support is negotiated again and again with each client in terms of a case-specific logic. The role of the therapist is therefore one of coaching and accompanying the client. The degree of intervention introduced by the therapist is a dynamic function based on the actual level of the client's autonomy, his or her biographic background, and the momentary necessities of a situation or social context. Interventions have to be negotiated with the client, thus permitting him or her to learn to manage social reality and assume personal responsibility.

The goal of this undertaking is to bring old patterns of experience to the surface of the mind so that one can work with them directly. At the same time it is necessary to gain distance from them so that one cannot be overpowered. For the clients, this becomes possible by the continuous practice of awareness and wisdom (of the changing nature of bodily sensations), with the aim of becoming free from harmful habits. At first, the old patterns are strong, but gradually they become less distinct until finally they dissolve completely, which means one can let go of them. This process of dissolving requires a great deal of perseverance and tolerance of frustration, because one cannot actually do anything to dissolve mental-somatic models except observe the natural flow of their arising and passing away. The crucial thing is to stay calm, stay aware, observe with equanimity, and wait, because, since everything by nature changes, harmful habits will dissolve automatically as long as they are not supported. By "supported" we mean reacting with craving and aversion to bodily sensations. If one reacts with craving and aversion, mental-somatic patterns do not dissolve, they multiply. Every reaction (craving, aversion) at the level of sensations is nutrition, but if these mental-somatic patterns are not fed, they have to dissolve over time. The Buddha described this process as a natural law (Dhammā), wherein mindfulness and awareness play a vital role in acknowledging and letting go. Before they can let go of them, however, practitioners (in our case, addicts) have to allow themselves to experience all their pain, ignorance, helplessness, and misery. This is important—the experience of "reality as it is" happens before anything is dissolved, and is the basic logic behind dissolving mental-somatic models successfully.

One important element of recovery from addiction is the concept "everyday life as therapy." Everything that occurs during the day is used to support and trigger therapeutic processes. This "everyday life" approach gives the client a feeling of calmness and respite, especially when combined with meetings with peers and self-help groups, and prepares the ground for other therapeutic processes in future—for example, clients learn to distinguish their everyday experience and its meaning, helping them to move away from blind reactions and preparing them for "plausible reasoning" in future decision-making (to borrow a term from the mathematician George Pólya (1990a, 1990b) who did extensive research on plausible reasoning). In this way the search for extraordinary ("peak") experiences within ordinary everyday life is confronted with reality—with what really is. Clients then no longer experience everyday life as boring and they are forced to accommodate themselves to their surroundings. Ideally, they are able to compare their subjective thought patterns of addiction with an everyday understanding of life. Addicts' typical thought patterns can be described as follows: "everything for free," "anxious about being in contact with other people," "excess," etc. The new thought patterns that now have to be learned and practiced are, e.g., "authenticity," "personal encounter," "frustration tolerance," etc. They actually attempt their first steps towards social integration, but for this they have to work on their motivation to maintain the goal of living a drug-free life (abstinence). They also need to reflect critically on their previous lifestyle.

As part of the concept of "therapy as everyday life," various therapeutic methods are available: individual systemic work, family therapy, marriage and couple counseling, biographic work, reflection of thought patterns and habitual actions, professional and social reintegration, etc. All these methods deal with addiction in a structured and methodical way. The whole complex aims at a structural transformation of the typical "either-or" pattern or attitude in thinking, feeling, and doing. Instead, a new, dynamic, and situationally changing pattern is learned, which can be called "both-and."

Taken together, these methods are, in turn, complemented and completed by the methodical meditative technique of self-observation at the level of bodily sensations. At first, only the technique of Ānāpāna-sati, concentration on the natural flow of breath coming in, breath coming out, is taught to stabilize the "monkey-mind" and allow an initial insight into the deep-rooted life patterns that were, and still are, responsible for the addiction. As described earlier, if clients are stabilized, they can also participate in a ten-day Vipassanā course. Practiced together properly, these techniques lead to the experience, at the level of bodily sensations, of dynamic reactions that can be summarized by the term "mental-somatic model." This new internal perspective makes it possible to establish the aforementioned attitude of "both-and," instead of "either-or." A practitioner of these techniques learns to stay calm regardless of what he or she experiences at the level of bodily sensations. This new composure is independent of the type of experience that occurs at any given time (pleasant sensations, unpleasant sensations), allows one to reflect new values, and gives access to very personal and subjective experiences related to understanding the "meaning" and "concept" of life—in short, engenders a new view of life. It is clear that this strongly supports every therapeutic process.

Two things are necessary for success: (1) establishing good contact with oneself, i.e., with one's bodily sensations, and (2) observing this process of being in contact mindfully and with great care. If there is just contact but no wisdom about how to encounter deep-rooted inner habits, they will not change because the right type of awareness is not established, i.e., mindfulness with equanimity. Conversely, if there is just equanimity but no specific contact, the deep-rooted habits will not come to the surface of the mind and be dissolved. In such a case, everything happens on the surface and, although on the surface there is peace and calm, this has no effect at all on the deep-rooted complexes of one's mental-somatic models. One has to go to the very depths of the mind to meet them and dissolve them little by little. For that reason, in Vipassanā, both awareness and wisdom are necessary and bound together.

The main task of the practice of Vipassanā is to bring about a change in blind mental reactions that are actually experienced at each moment at the level of bodily sensations. The link between craving for bodily sensations and addiction is revealed by the awareness of bodily sensations, and this awareness, when practiced with equanimity, is what provides, in that moment, a degree of freedom from mental desire, i.e., freedom from addiction. Addiction can, therefore, be seen as an addiction to physical sensations, whereas external substances (i.e., drugs) are merely the cause of the arising of the object of addiction, namely, ordinary physical bodily sensations. Reviewing the process of addiction, there are two options for further development: a spiral movement downwards or upwards. If the movement is downwards, the habitual tendency of "action (consume) justifies action (consume)" will harden and solidify (see definition of addiction by D.F. Wallace in section 3.1). If the movement is upwards, this tendency will weaken and action free from desire becomes possible.

The In-depth Systemics approach is not limited to addiction therapy. Indeed, as a support it has been broadened into various areas in which people need help. "Help" in this regard is not just for those who in their lives are confronted with enormous problems. The basic assumption is that everyone can learn something to improve one's life skills. But this "help for self-help" should be done in a methodical way. In the long run, everything is aimed at freeing the individual from mental-somatic models that prevent him or her from seeing reality "as it is," and not "as one would like it to be." It is particularly advantageous for people who are in positions of responsibility and need to make wise decisions; for these people, the In-depth Systemics approach will demonstrate how to decide based on the exigencies of a given situation. Thus, areas of application for In-depth Systemics are widespread: in health care, in fostering cooperation, for letting go of dysfunctional thought patterns, in working to free oneself from mental projections, etc. In-depth Systemics assists not only "clients," but also professionals, therapists, counselors, coaches, executives, and managers. Why is it so broad in its application? Because the concept is totally systemic in nature: one can help with an object only insofar as one has already mastered the same object. In this sense In-depth Systemics has been further developed by the company "mensch und organisation" (m&o[18]) in the areas of organizational learning, case management and health care, sports and athletic ability, personality development, and human resources development.

6.5 Current model of In-depth Systemics

From the explanations above, we can see that the core element of In-depth Systemics is helping people gain a higher degree of personal autonomy by fostering self-help to abstain from craving, aversion, and ego through the practice of Vipassanā meditation. However, the In-depth Systemics model contains many elements besides the practice of dealing with bodily sensations. It is not sufficient just to teach addicts Vipassanā ; there are too many other problems in their daily social lives. They are frequently short on life skills, and in most cases do not have jobs or proper job training. In short, there is a lot clients have to work on besides addiction.

Thus the In-depth Systemics model shown in figure 6.1 has been developed further into a double pyramid as can be seen in figure 6.2. Although Vipassanā still plays a central role in the model, there are other elements that must be considered. In-depth Systemics is not identical to Vipassanā . Vipassanā is an individual spiritual discipline and In-depth Systemics is embedded in a social context, and has to be adapted to that context to serve those who expect benefits from it. Since its inception, the In-depth Systemics model has been molded and adapted in the light of ongoing research and evaluation. Below, we briefly review the current model as shown in figure 6.2. In addition, there are reasons why this model is not only capable of helping addicts to become "better at what they are doing," but other people too. As we have stated above, although In-depth Systemics was developed in addiction therapy, it is now a general model for helping people along their life trajectory and with their current state of mind.

The three main elements of the In-depth Systemics approach are shown as the three edges of the base of the pyramid (see figure 6.2):

1. Reconstructive work,
2. Coopetition (defined below), and
3. Skills, abilities, and qualifications.

A fourth element additionally integrates the other three elements: the right mental attitude necessary to deal with what is actually experienced from moment to moment on the level of bodily sensations. This fourth element—the spiral in figure 6.2—is the practice of Vipassanā .

1. *Reconstructive work.* This covers all aspects of biographic work, family work, past experiences, etc. Reconstructive work is dedicated to resolving the underlying structures that dominate one's life pattern. The process involves identifying problem areas as well as resources, and then deciding how to deal with or use them. Of course, deficiencies should be diminished and resources accumulated and expanded. Furthermore, potentials

Basic model of In-depth Systemics

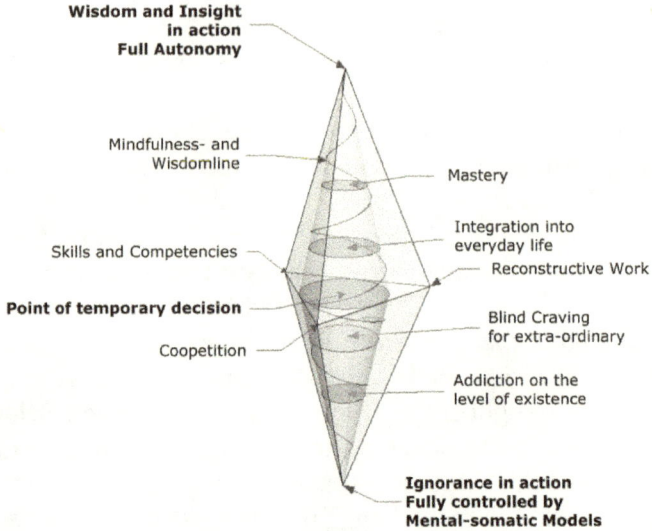

Figure 6.2: *Current model of the In-depth Systemics approach*

should be uncovered, activated, and cultivated. At first, this is only an ideal, and in practice does not typically unfold the way one might expect. It is a nonlinear process of progress and (temporary) regression.

2. *Coopetition.* This term describes the interplay of competition and cooperation that underlies all social interactions. It covers all aspects of social life, regardless of context—friends, other professionals, or peers (i.e., in our case, other addicts). In our social lives we are always eager to express our own thoughts about how we think life should be. We try hard because we want our ideas to be applied; however, if everyone we meet does the same, we are all confronted at the same time with various different world views. Then there are two options: either we maintain our own opinions (i.e., the mode of competition), or we neglect our own opinions in order to cooperate. If we choose the first option, in the long run we become socially isolated (realistically, there is only a very, very small chance that our

thoughts and decisions are always the best choice of all the possibilities). On the other hand, if we neglect our own opinions and only cooperate, we become dissatisfied. We have to learn to integrate both aspects—cooperation as well as competition—and only in this area of conflict can we discover new solutions and perspectives. This, in general, is a fundamental aspect of social life. In the case of addicts, self-help groups and the post- or re-socialization process of learning to live with peers and to support each other is a good example of coopetition.

3. *Skills, abilities, and qualifications.* In order to manage their lives, people need various skills and qualifications. Being able to do something is not the same as being a good performer. Everyone can learn something new in his or her field of interest (job, profession, social life, sports, etc.) and become a better performer. In the case of addiction, addicts have to learn to live a normal life. Therefore they need the skills necessary to maintain a daily structure, establish and maintain social relationships, and care for their bodies. They also need to learn various life skills such as reading, writing, mathematics and, in many cases, start and/or finish a training so that they are employable (again).

The cones in the middle of the pyramids demonstrate the two potentials for future development: integration and disintegration. The whole model represents a picture, a snapshot, of a highly dynamic process, which, in reality, changes from moment to moment. Every moment one can choose whether to act as a consequence of craving, aversion, or ego—or not. If actions are performed based on craving, aversion, or ego, then addiction at the basic level of existence (i.e., bodily sensations) occurs and dominates life. If actions are, instead, based on wisdom and free from craving, aversion, or ego, everything conforms to reality, regardless of previous problems and current obstacles. Only the present moment is important because it is the only time when decisions can be made and actions performed. However, all long-range efforts will and should be directed towards the goal of integration into daily life. What is important is not a top-notch performance, which is a rare event, but a performance that typically leads to some progress each day.

The two tips of the double pyramid (upper and lower) illustrate two contrasting states. The upper tip represents the developmental ideal: "wisdom in action" or "full autonomy," which can be characterized by the total absence of mental-somatic models. Actions are not based on craving, aversion, or ego, and the three elements mentioned above (reconstructive work, coopetition, and skills and abilities) combine in the natural flow of life and together unfold their combined potency. This does not mean that no difficult obstacles or incidents occur in life, but the individual has all the abilities necessary to retain a balance of mind. Reality is seen "as it is," and not as one thinks it should be, and actions are always in line with actual necessities. Everything outside the pyramid happens naturally and without a need to plan. The meditation practice easily becomes a normal habit, and one lives in full harmony with nature itself.

The counterpart on the lower tip is "ignorance in action" or "no autonomy at all." One is controlled externally by one's deep-rooted mental-somatic models and is a slave to one's own desires. Reality is not recognized for what it is, and potentials can neither be activated nor cultivated. Even if one makes effort, results may not be seen. Still, this very effort is the only way to come out of ignorance, develop the three elements (reconstructive work, coopetition, and skills and abilities), and improve one's life. Continuous effort and proper practice are the keys to success, even if it takes a very long time. When one has lived for 20 years or so addicted to drugs, it takes considerable time and effort to overcome all the misery sown day by day. This is simply a matter of cause and effect.

Of course, a model is only a model and, as stated above, not static. Each moment its elements will vary. Each moment one has to choose how to act and to deal with all the experiences that arise. Each moment there is a chance to break past habits, try something new, or change for the better. This has to be done regardless of the type of experiences that occur. They may be unpleasant, such as a difficulty in life or a failure, or pleasant like success or acclaim, but the proper mental attitude in every case is to remain calm and realistic about oneself and all the contextual variables (persons, situations, issues, etc.). The same is true in other applications, whether one is working on one's biography as part of addiction therapy, or is a professional learning how to improve—it doesn't matter: the structure of the practice is exactly the same. Each individual has to learn something and, in so doing, meets obstacles from the past that can derail progress and blunt potential. There are, of course, great differences between addicts and other types of clients or professionals. The level at which they start their work is, for example, in most cases quite different. One may have access to reliable resources, whereas another may encounter only deficiencies. Disparities have to be accepted as they are. In addition, there may also be limits that one is not be able to transcend at a given moment, or that may last for a very long time (or at least for this lifetime). As we mentioned earlier, continuous effort is the key to success for whatever can be attained. If one wants to learn to play the piano, one has to practice properly and continuously. That is all.

Notes

15. Narcotics Anonymous: www.na.org

16. Rational Recovery Systems: https://rational.org

17. www.dhamma.org

18. www.muo.ch

The necessity of reasoning as best we can in situations where our information is incomplete is faced by all of us, every waking hour of our lives. We must decide what to do next, even though we cannot be certain what the consequences will be.

Bayesian Methods: General Background
Edwin T. Jaynes

Evaluation

7.1 The start again evaluation study, 1995–98

Between 1995 and 1998, start againwas scientifically evaluated by one of the authors (Studer, 1998). This evaluation was supported financially as a "model project" by the Swiss Government (Department of Justice/ Bundesamt für Justiz). The data analyzed ranged from 1992 to 1998. The evaluation report can be freely downloaded from the start again's website or from the website of the Swiss Department of Justice.[19]

The principal aim of the evaluation was to investigate clients' typical odds of success from the application of the In-depth Systemics approach to drug therapy. On the basis of individual case studies and by making use of Objective Hermeneutics—a qualitative casereconstructive method developed by Oevermann et al. (1979) which was already discussed in section 4.1—individual structures of drug dependence and the basic process of becoming addicted were explored.

Additionally, the quantitative and qualitative data were combined to provide an overall summary. Quantitative data were analyzed by methods of Bayesian statistics (Gill, 2008; Bolstad, 2007; Gregory,

2006). This class of statistical techniques was further developed in the 20th century by the physicist Edwin T. Jaynes (2003) in the tradition of Bernoulli, Bayes, Laplace, Jeffreys, and Pólya. Bayesian statistics allow the integration of qualitative information into quantitative equations (Studer, 1996, 2006), which makes it possible to analyze data precisely and with consistent conclusions in cases where sample sizes are very small, as is often the case for clinical evaluation studies. As a result, meaningful conclusions can be drawn. The basic procedure stands in the tradition of plausible reasoning (Pólya, 1990a, 1990b)[20].

The overall results demonstrate that the clients investigated were in most characteristics equivalent to those in the FOS[21] reference framework for clients in the 1990's. Slight differences were found—namely, start again's clients were less likely to be women, tended to be from large cities with a higher socioeconomic status, and were less traumatized by past experiences of violence in their families of origin and therefore demonstrated healthier social relationships with family members. start again's clients also showed less drug use (except for nicotine and cocaine) and had more previous experiences with psychotherapy. They also, to a greater extent, encountered problems with the law, thus more convictions came across in this sample. The last characteristic is an expression of the high number of start again clients that chose a program called "therapy instead of prison."

Quite interesting are the self-reports and reasons given by these clients as to why they chose to take part in drug therapy: e.g., "to lead a better and more conscious life," "self-fulfillment," "drugs don't solve problems," and "anxiety about future mental and physical damage." External rationales such as problems with the law or serious difficulties at work, school, etc., were not predominant, nor was pressure and urging by those from diffuse social relationships like friends, partners, or parents. These latter reasons proved not to be crucial in making the decision to stop using drugs and to start a therapeutic process. Thus, the goal of start again—reintegration of personal identity and autonomy—encompasses these clients and their motives fairly reasonably. While these responses add to our understanding of the underlying motivation for participation in drug therapy, one has to remember, however, as we mentioned earlier, that motivation is at first a manifestation of interests. Motivation for withdrawal or for therapy is not a static condition but a dynamic process, changing repeatedly through the long and profound process of drug therapy: in addicts, there is sometimes more of it present, and sometimes less. Sometimes it works on the surface and sometimes it is hidden, latent among many layers of past experience and dispositions for various actions. At any given moment, it is a complex variable based on biographic involvement and dynamic interaction with environmental variables. As a result, motivation can be understood only by a precise individual case analysis over a long period of time. However, this characteristic is not only true for addicts but for many people who wish to change their deep rooted life patterns.

The catamnestic period ranged from half a year up to five years. The evaluation study distinguished among various degrees of success. The criteria for success were divided into Full Success, Indifferent Success, and No Success. Full Success meant clients abstained from hard drugs and did not consume soft drugs excessively. Additionally, they must not have had problems with the law and must have followed a regular daily structure. Furthermore, it was also required that former clients maintained social relationships, had some kind of accommodation, and—most importantly—continued the process of working on the dissolution of their addiction, i.e., had attended NA/RRS meetings, taken Vipassanā courses and practiced regularly at home, or visited a therapist for post-treatment. All these points are indicators of a relative increase in personal autonomy.

Indifferent Success occurred either if not enough information was available about clients, or they did not consume hard drugs but did not perform the personal contribution activities described above. No Success meant cases of relapse or regular consumption of hard drugs. In almost all cases this also meant that these clients were not able to maintain regular social relationships. There was also a high likelihood of problems with the law in relation to drug purchases. If all the results are taken together, the overall summary shows that in 1998 about two-thirds of clients could be categorized as having a " relative increase in personal autonomy." This is, proportionately, a high rate, and not just for the field of addiction.[22]

Another positive result is the fact that "nonvoluntary" clients from the "therapy instead of prison" program had the same success rates as ordinary "voluntary" clients. Experience also shows that the political conditions and framework play an important role. A rough measure of this issue is the length of stay: the longer clients are in therapy, the greater their chances of successful rehabilitation. Additionally, the danger of a serious relapse is diminished to the same extent. Due to the characteristics of the "therapy instead of prison" program, the longer stay can compensate the initial motivation of such clients which may be more extrinsic than intrinsic motivated. Therefor these clients can gain the same benefit as voluntary clients. There were no significant differences between men and women; both gained the same benefits from the program.

If systemic family therapy is explored as an isolated factor, there are no differences to be found whether addicts take part in family talks during therapy or not. However, this seeming lack of incongruity becomes much clearer if the systemic framework approach of start again is taken into consideration. For example, as a consequence of the therapeutic program every client undergoes serious biographic work and takes part in a precise reconstructive work of his or her addiction. This means that every client undergoes strong family work; however, only one part entails taking part in family discussions or couples counseling, other parts can be done alone without the presence of family members.

Lastly, we add the finding that taking part in a ten-day Vipassanā course is not a general predictor of success, but is a highly significant predictor of prevention of a serious relapse. Thus the practice of Vipassanā does play a crucial role, especially in the management of crises, and is a valuable resource before incidents lead to renewed drug consumption. On the other hand, clients who attend a Vipassanā course are, to some extent, those who already have greater resources and are often more likely fit for a course. During a course, participants are continuously confronted with themselves and with their mental-somatic models. This is almost always a very hard time for them, but it does not guarantee that they are working on their addiction at the depths of the mind. Thus, just taking part in a tenday course is not a predictor of success, per se, and this was mirrored in the quantitative analyses mentioned above. There is no causal relationship between participation and continuous self-confrontation. However, there is a better chance that clients will work on their addictions as a result of a Vipassanā course than without one. Ten days is a long time, during which there are many opportunities to try out the meditation technique.

Furthermore, mere participation does not guarantee that the technique is understood properly, nor that its practice will lead to the cessation of harmful mental-somatic models. Continuity of practice, however, provided that it is performed correctly, enhances the chances of grasping the technique and thereby gaining considerable benefit. But this work has to be maintained after therapy—one of the greatest obstacles, not just for every client but for every practitioner of Vipassanā. In the long run, progress is toward structural transformation, a realistic view of life, and a new basic assumption: in case of uncertainty, everything will go well. We call this point of view "realistic developmental optimism."

While the finding that attending a ten-day Vipassanā course is not a general predictor of success, because Vipassanā must still be considered an integral part of the whole program. It does not make sense—from a systemic point of view—to isolate the separate factors of the program (Vipassanā , family talks, etc.) and estimate their contribution as isolated agents of success—although this *is* possible by the straightforward application of statistics. However, it does have to be done, for example for political reasons. And, since it was done for the evaluation of start again, the results were reported above: Vipassanā is not a predictor of success, but of preventing relapse.

The program as a whole must be evaluated and this was done successfully. In sum, we can announce that the program does work and leads to success (as defined above) in a high proportion of cases. Due to recurring political debates about whether it makes sense to promote abstinence-oriented drug therapy or not, we have to state: yes, it not only makes sense but actually works. Such programs should therefore be fostered instead of barred. This does not mean that there are no clients at all for whom a drug substitution program is the better choice at a specific time in their lives. But this choice has to be reconsidered from time to time so that those addicts do get an opportunity in future to lead a life totally free from drugs and harmful substances. On a social and political level, abstinence-oriented programs not only contribute to individual quality of life, but in the long run are also cost-effective and therefore make a much greater contribution to the wealth and wellbeing of society as whole.

If we try to isolate the core factors of start again that contribute to success, we still conclude and repeat that it is the program *as a whole* that leads to success and no isolated factors predominate. We call this concept "In-depth Systemics." In line with Aristotelian thinking—that the whole is more than the sum of its parts—In-depth Systemics is a concept that must be adopted in its contextual parts but works as a totality. If it works the right way, it pushes and triggers potential in people whether they are addicts, artists, athletes, professionals, etc. (for more detail on this issue see Gürtler, Studer, and Scholz,

2010). This implies that the concept cannot be transferred one-on-one from context to context; it has to be integrated into its context of application. It does not have to be created from scratch every time, but it must be assembled using various elements like the building blocks in the double pyramid of In-depth Systemics described above. In the authors' book, this issue is discussed at greater length.

Notes

19. www.startagain.ch/files/Fallstudie_Vollversion.pdf

20. This kind of data-handling is located on the frontier between purely quantitative and purely qualitative data analysis, and represents a real integration of both research strategies (Studer, 2006). The comparison of the various groups was operationally realized by an algorithm developed by G.L. Bretthorst (1993), published in his article "On the Difference in Means." The paper describes a totally new approach to solving the Behrens-Fisher problem, which is, in fact, the two-sample problem (i.e., difference in means and difference in standard deviations of two samples). The implementation was done for Mathematica and for R (www.r-project.org). Both are obtainable from the authors.

21. The FOS (In German: 'Forschungsverbund stationäre Suchttherapie' in der Schweiz) is a research association for inpatient drug therapy in Switzerland, which has set up a reference framework for comparisons.

22. However, since that time, the success rate has fallen somewhat due to the dramatic increase in co-morbidities (mostly personality disorders) and heavy polytoxic drug consumption. Between 2000 and 2006, it was about 50%.

And te tide and te time þat tu iboren were, schal beon iblescet. (Time and opportunity wait for no man.)

St. Marher, 1225

Catamnestic findings

I f we want to understand the process of recovery from addiction better, it is always a good idea to perform a catamnestic study. Accordingly, such a study was conducted by one of the authors (Gürtler). Five former clients from start again, classified in the evaluation study as Full Success, were chosen for investigation. Several interviews with each of them were conducted and the topics covered included all the important incidents of their lives that had taken place since their stay at start again. The interviews were transcribed and analyzed using the qualitative method of Objective Hermeneutics.

8.1 Principles of recovery

From the general results of the research study, three structural principles were identified. Although these factors are still hypotheses, they do at least have heuristic value in describing the process of recovery from addiction. They are:

1. the principle of small steps,
2. the principle of small changes, and
3. the principle of changing the sign.

There is also a fourth principle that will only be introduced later because it was not found in the cases analyzed. For now, let us look at these three principles.

1. The *principle of small steps* reminds us that, if a client has been living an addict's life for a long period, we cannot expect recovery within weeks or even months. Every step that has to be taken in life should be of such a size that a client can manage it successfully. Here a potential problem might

arise: the projection of a therapist's assumptions when s/he presumes to know better than the client. Although we do not at all think that clients are always capable of knowing what is really good for them, we likewise retain serious doubts whether therapists necessarily know better. In In-depth Systemics, it is always critical for therapists to confront their own mental-somatic models and biographical burdens. What is true for clients is also true for professionals: mental projections are mental projections. If therapists master this successfully, they are considerably more capable of seeing their clients as they really are, leading naturally to planning each client's steps in accordance with actual capabilities. There is no shame in planning tiny steps if they conform correctly to the client's potential for development. In psychological terms this is called "adaptive learning." To help understand this complex process, we take a pragmatic analogy from martial arts. To teach agaility, a master repeatedly throws (metaphorical) stones between the legs of his students according to the capacity of the student. The stones must be of such a size that the student is just barely capable of dodging them. If the stone is too big, the student will become frustrated by the effort and may stop learning. If the stone is too small, the student, already knowing how to dodge small stones, won't learn anything. The stones must be neither too big nor too small, just big enough to handle—the middle path. Adaptive learning is a process of dynamic moment-to-moment social interaction, and surely one of the most delicate jobs in psychotherapy—and in social interaction in general.

2. The *principle of small changes* is a consequence of the first principle. Therapeutic success *can* be attained; however, it requires that therapists work continuously, patiently, and with adequate effort to provide and offer a developmental context. It is also necessary to create a learning space in which to work, and to frame suitable learning contexts according to the needs and capabilities of the client. This has to be done even if no obvious sign points to any chance of success. Our experience clearly demonstrates that success does not follow a linear relationship with effort or any other indicator one may choose to adopt. With some clients, it sometimes seems that success (defined operationally as a relative increase in autonomy) is not possible at all, in either the near or distant future. But then,

unexpectedly, dramatic changes occur within a very short time and a therapeutic success, as defined above, will manifest. At other times an assumed success is actually not progress, but regress. These findings can be summed up by the term "professional waiting," that is, staying with clients through all their efforts and failures during the entire therapeutic process, which, at every step, is led by the individual case structure and its professional reconstruction. Unforeseen openings and small changes that point to possible developments have to be used immediately as they occur. This requires mindfulness as well as continuous concentration on the part of the therapists. They have to learn for themselves to be patient and aware, but also ready to act at the right moment without hesitation and with confidence in their own competency. The non-linearity of the relationship of intervention and consequences makes the process unpredictable for professionals—but small changes can, in the long run, lead to substantial and stable changes that remain effective for a client for prolonged periods.

3. The *principle of changing the sign* refers to the fact that almost any vulnerability can be structurally transformed into a resource. What was harmful in the past—dysfunctional thoughts, destructive habits, unhealthy relationships, etc.— can be a resource of great strength in future, Things are not what they seem to be; rather, they are what one makes of them. Things can be used for good or ill. Furthermore, it is the underlying mental intention and not the obvious action that counts. It is up to the therapist (and the client) to choose wisely. An example is given below in the excerpts from the catamnestic case studies. However, to apply this principle in life takes a long time, because one has to reflect on and confront previous experiences and strong patterns of action. This can also imply—in the case of vulnerabilities—a very difficult and painful process. We are very uncertain whether this process can be planned sequentially like principles (1) and (2). Rather, it is very plausible that (3) is a consequence of the hard work already done in (1) and (2). Then, specific underlying patterns change so that people can see things from another perspective. The practice of Vipassanā is extremely helpful in this process because it adds another dimension: the world within, the world of normal, ordinary, bodily sensations. The observation of bodily

sensations reveals not only the link between body and mind, but also our habitual reactions to these sensations: desire, craving, and aversion.

There is a fourth principle, described in the teachings of the Buddha and experienced by some Vipassanā meditators, that we shall call the *principle of dissolution*. This principle, a consequence of (3), the *principle of changing the sign*, was not realized by any in the investigated sample (it is a lofty step for anyone, not just addicts!). According to this principle, the sign is actually not changed, but the object of the principle is dissolved completely, and, if something has vanished completely, it cannot do any more harm. As a result, a person is free from that particular bondage. This does not necessarily mean that the strength of the object of principle (3) is lost, for if a deficit is transformed into a resource, it is still a resource according to (4)—it does not get lost. It just means that people gain more autonomy in a much greater sense than by merely changing the sign: they gain independence in the sense that their mind remains stable whether a resource or even a deficit is present or not—a crucial breakthrough. Actually, this is the ultimate goal of Vipassanā —to eradicate mental-somatic models altogether, not just transform them into something harmless.

8.2 Excerpts from the case studies

We cite here some interesting details from the catamnestic case studies to clarify the principles introduced above, and their underlying structure. For example, with regard to principle (3), elevated cognitive abilities (i.e., a high Intelligence Quotient) can be a vulnerability factor if this high IQ is substantially disconnected from practical aspects of life. An example is the case of Beat Kaiser (not his real name; see more details of this case in Studer, 1998, chapter 3.2) whose superior IQ unfortunately contributed to his social status as an outsider in his earlier social life. His biographic background shows that he lost his father when he was a very young and his relationship with his mother was problematic. As a small child he experienced a traumatic stay in hospital for several months, during which time he was unable to move his body or play with his peers. His long hospital stay, the social exclusion by his peers that ensued, and, later, his great height, all contributed to his establishing his identity as an outsider even before he started taking drugs. As a young man, he demonstrated his outsider status by his attitudes, by taking drugs, by his overall life style, etc. During his stay at start again

Beat was famous, and infamous, for his cynicism. Every encounter was difficult for all involved. He (mis)used his intellect to undercut the general rules of the institution and to demonstrate that every rule has an exception.

During the catamnestic interviews, his cynicism seemed not as harsh as it was in the past when he was in treatment. It appeared that he used his superior intellect and cynicism as shields to cloak his fragile emotions. Previously there had been no place for altruism, but now this pattern had changed substantially. Although he still used cynicism, altruism was also present—not so much in his words but in his actions. After leaving start againBeat obained certain qualifications as a social worker and began working with addicts.[23] While working with addicts he changed his mind, and during our interviews he talked about plans to work in future with the handicapped—which we interpret as a structural transformation based on the experience of altruism and caring for others. He not only demonstrated that he had really worked on dissolving his addiction (e.g., by staying abstinent), but also evinced a clear intention to leave the context of addiction altogether (but not the context of social work). Compared to many former addicts who cannot leave the addiction context, this is atypical behavior.

Beat's elevated intellectual skills allowed him to study social work after treatment. He was accepted at a college of higher education without a proper lower-school certificate, and passed the entrance examination on his first attempt—incredible, considering 20 years of heavy drug consumption! His cognitive abilities were no longer a vulnerability or an obstacle; they had *changed the sign* and now supported him as a solid resource. His perception of himself as an outsider altered, too: he experienced himself as a person properly integrated into social life, and became involved in a relationship with a deaf woman. Because she was deaf, his verbal cynicism could not reach her. It also meant (to him) that he was engaging with another kind of outsider.[24]

Being engaged to someone he saw as physically handicapped, as he saw himself handicapped by his own body, allowed him to continue his outsider lifestyle under a new sign. His plan to stop working with addicts and work with the handicapped can be understood as a legitimate attempt truly to overcome addiction. This was not something based on his previous efforts, but on the experience of "what it is like" to be an outsider—really something new. His implicit discovery of acting altruistically opened a hidden window for his intellect: not to do harm, but to do good in a field of social outsiders. We assume that if he continues in this direction in future, his intellect will not only be of great benefit in his professional work, but also less of an issue. His intellect will just be a part of him, like the many other facets of his personality—a really great step toward a relative increase in autonomy.

Another example demonstrating the *principle of changing the sign* is found in the case of Natalie Lang (also not her real name; see more details in Studer, 1998, appendix A.3). The structure in her case was called "outsourcing excessiveness" (i.e., of feelings and emotions). Her family milieu was "silent," a petty bourgeois world with a highly structured social environment. There were no "voices," no expressions of feelings or emotions, and topics relevant to the life of the family were never communicated verbally (see Studer, 1998, for more details). Her particular vulnerability was identified as the lack of an emotional relationship with her parents. Following her treatment at start again, she married a man from Africa, but they divorced after a short time. She then had a daughter with another African to whom she was not married. For various reasons (maintenance of the child, breakup of the relationship with the father of her daughter, etc.), she moved near her parents and reestablished a relationship with them. According to Natalie, this was only possible because of the family talks she had had at start again. She was able to maintain her family links for several years after treatment, and her parents were very happy to have their daughter and granddaughter near them. They supported Nathalie with both their time and energy which permitted her to find employment. She, in turn, really appreciated her parent's efforts and her new closeness to them. She no longer consumed hard or soft drugs, though she still drank alcohol in moderation. Although emotions and vital activities were still not a part of family encounters, Natalie no longer felt a need to produce an alternative lifestyle to that of her parents. Thus, the previously problematic relationship with her family changed from a vulnerability to an important resource for all of them, and her previous handicaps changed into factors for resilience. Although the milieu of the family is still "silent" to some nebulous degree, nonetheless it now provides stability and reliability. Perhaps the "silence" too has changed from a threatening aspect of family life to a resource—in the sense that silence allows for recovery, provides peace, etc. And we should not underestimate the power of the presence of a new family member. Natalie's daughter surely turns the silence into life—but in a natural and healthy way.

We do not think that the solutions described above can, in therapy, be systematically planned as part of a normal process—they just reflect life as it happens. But to have them happen requires a lot of previous hard work and effort, much of it occuring within a therapeutic framework. Solutions therefore are both a consequence of hard work, and gifts from life itself, not planned results.

Unfortunately, other case studies demonstrate that sometimes the effects of abstinence from drugs, along with obviously increased relative autonomy, are only temporary. Progress might be for a limited time only, and therefore not stable. We know many life stories in which, as a consequence of renewed stressful life circumstances, old and harmful habits resurface. Hidden, but still-existent, mechanisms of avoidance of being out of alignment take over in such cases. Unable to cope with overwhelming incidents and experiences, some clients start retaking drugs. This does not mean, however, that they have lost every possibility of future recovery. There is always another chance to start again. In these cases another cycle of recovery work is necessary to reach the next level of stability and abstinence from drugs. Although it will be very difficult, another relative increase in personal autonomy can be attained. This cyclic process of progress and regress is not the exception, but a regular and quite typical rule in the addiction recovery process, and is witnessed repeatedly in practice.

Notes

23. This represents a common pattern in many ex-addicts who assume, because they were addicts, that they know exactly how to treat addicts successfully—a highly problematic professional attitude, but we shall not discuss this topic at length here.

24. This does not mean that the authors consider the deaf to be outsiders. Here we are merely reporting Beat's perspective from his biography, not our perspective nor that of his girlfriend.

How wonderful it is that nobody need wait a single moment
before starting to improve the world.

———————————

Anne Frank

Conclusion

At the end of this essay we want to express some additional thoughts about the phenomenon of chronic relapse that is typical with every addiction—and not only with addiction, but also with other attempts to change life patterns in general. Regardless of whether people try to be less angry, less anxious, etc., all will sometimes fall back into old thoughts, old habits, and harmful patterns of reaction. Even though drug addiction usually has decidedly more serious consequences than being anxious, the subjective experience of misery can be much the same. So we cannot conclude that one problem is necessarily worse than another. A problem is a problem, and to overcome a problem takes time, effort, and the wisdom to surmount difficulties. For this reason it makes sense to distinguish within the In-depth Systemics approach between prolapse (incident) and relapse (regression).

If clients (re)consume drugs, this just means that their coping mechanisms and their personal autonomy have reached their limits at this very moment. Routines fail and crisis emerges. We do not know what will happen in future and, as stated above, such a relapse can happen after a long period of abstinence and a turning away from the social context of drugs. Again reaching the limits of their autonomy, clients reinstate their old habits of faking, masking, and inscrutability, which triggers an experience of shame. If a drug is then taken (again), we want to decide precisely whether this is relapse or prolapse. To do so, we look at the type of conflict clients undergo when confronted with their consumption. If they are able to make use of the experience to discover something new about themselves, to understand how it happened, to plan new and realistic steps for the future, etc., we assume they are able to learn from the experience and we call it prolapse. If clients avoid self-confrontation and discussion, and if they are not willing to work on their habits and mental-somatic models, then we call it relapse. The framework for this decision is prepared by a one-to-three weeks' residence in a rehab clinic or within a social-pedagogical, shared-apartment community. Clients undergo a time-out to think about their motivation for therapy. During this interval they have time to write a prolapse paper which is reported and critically discussed with peers in a plenum. The reporting of each individual's biographical work of addiction is within the same frame-work: plenum, peers, and critical discussion. Clients are urged to construct a theme within their prolapse work involving not only their anxieties, difficulties, and doubts, but also their hopes, resources, and confidence for recovery. Recovery from addiction is not a linear process; it is, on the contrary, nonlinear, divided into many cyclic phases that sometimes seem to be repeated under identical conditions. This repetitiveness is actually an illusion since there are no identical conditions, but there are, almost always, near-identical structures present that continue to exert great influence on thinking, feeling, and doing. This has to be carefully considered for every case.

Handling relapses as well as prolapses is part of the strategy to help addicts live a better life. Putting aside for the moment the underlying structure of addiction, relapse can, to some extent, be regarded as a simple problem of noncompliance with therapeutic rules or the therapeutic process. The problem of "compliance" can be discussed from various perspectives. We cite an interesting paper written by Nash (1997), in which the author discusses the problem of compliance rates in the context of addiction and other medical problems and diseases:

> "Ironically, the biggest barrier to making such care [i.e., the therapy of addicted clients] available is the perception that efforts to treat addiction are wasted. Yet treatment for drug abuse has a failure rate no different from that for other chronic diseases. Close to half of recovering addicts fail to maintain complete abstinence after a year [which is] about the same proportion of patients with diabetes and hypertension who fail to comply with their diet, exercise, and medication regimens."

There is very little doubt in the public mind that the treatment of diabetes or high blood pressure is imperative—even if patients are noncompliant. No one would seriously contemplate not attending to these patients because—for whatever reason—they do not take their pills, or they stop injecting themselves with insulin, or they are unable to stick to their diets. However, these classes of patients have the same compliance rates as addicts. Furthermore, there is a great deal of research to develop treatment programs for patients with high blood pressure, diabetes, etc., to increase their compliance rates, and to help them take more responsibility for themselves. The same must be done for addicts in addiction therapy.

Finally, let us return to the beginning of modern psychology at the end of the 19th century and beginning of the 20th. In 1904, after listening to a guest talk about Buddhist psychology at Harvard University, the great psychologist and pragmatist William James (1842–1910) announced: "This is the psychology everybody will be studying 25 years from now" (Thompson, 2006; see also Fields, 1981, p.134ff.). Unfortunately, that did not happen. Perhaps James was overly optimistic about his generation. However, reflecting on the urgent need to overcome our own mental-somatic models and to dissolve our entanglements, not just at some time in future but here and now, we hope that by integrating the ancient wisdom of Vipassanā and the modern approaches of therapy and counseling, the In-depth Systemics approach will contribute somewhat toward the eventual realization of James' prophecy.

Bibliography

Bennett, M. & Hacker, P. (2003). *Philosophical Foundations of Neuroscience.* Oxford: Blackwell Publishers. 35

Berridge, K. (2005). Espresso reward learning, hold the dopamine: Theoretical comment on Robinson et al. (2005). *Behavioral Neuroscience*, 119 (1), 336–341. 35

Berridge, K. (2007). The debate over dopamine's role in reward: The case for incentive salience. *Psychopharmacology*, 191, 391–431. 31, 35

Berridge, K., Flynn, F., Schulkin, J., & Grill, H. (1984). Sodium depletion enhances salt palatability in rats. *Behavioral Neuroscience*, 98, 652–660. 31

Berridge, K. & Kringelbach, M. (2008). Affective neuroscience of pleasure: Reward in humans and animals. *Psychopharmacology*, 199, 457–480. 31

Berridge, K., Robinson, T., & Aldrige, J. (2009). Dissecting components of reward: »liking«, »wanting«, and »learning«. *Current Opinion in Pharmacology*, 9, 65–73. 31

Bolstad, W. (2007). *Introduction to Bayesians Statistics.* Hoboken, New Jersey: John Wiley and Sons, Inc. 65

Bretthorst, G. (1993). On the difference in means. In W. Grandy & P. Milonni (Eds.), *Physics and Probability Essays in honor of Edwin T. Jaynes* (pp. 177–194). Cambridge: Cambridge University Press. http://bayes.wustl. edu/glb/diff.pdf. 70

Buddhist Publication Society, Ed. (1985). *The Dhammā pada. The Buddha's Path of Wisdom. Translated from the Pā li by Ācariya Buddharakkhita.* Kandy, Sri Lanka. http://www.accesstoinsight.org/tipitaka/kn/dhp/index.html. 36

Damasio, A. (1999). *Ich fühle, also bin ich.* München: Econ Ullstein List Verlag. 34

Damasio, A. R. (1994). *Descartes' Irrtum — Fühlen, Denken und das menschliche Gehirn.* München: List Verlag. 34

Di Chiara, G. (1995a). Psychobiology of the role of dopamine in drug abuse and addiction. *Neurosci. Res. Commun.*, 17, 133–143. 34

Di Chiara, G. (1995b). The role of dopamine in drug abuse viewed from the perspective of its role in motivation. *Drug and Alcohol Dep.*, 38, 95–137. 34

Fields, R. (1981). *How the swans came to the lake: A narrative history of Buddhism in America.* Boston: Shambala. 85

Gershon, M. (2001). *Der kluge Bauch. Die Entdeckung des zweiten Gehirns.* München: Goldmann. 35

Gill, J. (2008). *Bayesian methods. A social and behavioral sciences approach.* London: Chapman and Hall/ CRC. 65

Goenka, S. N. (1991). Abendvorträge eines 10-Tage-Kurses in Vipassanā meditation. http://www.dhamma.org. 36, 37, 49

Goenka, S. N. (1997). *The discourse summaries.* Igatpuri, India: V.R.I. 36, 37

Goenka, S. N. (1998). *Satipaṭṭhāna Sutta Discourses by S.N. Goenka.* Seattle, Washington: Vipassanā Research Publications. 36, 37, 39, 49

Gregory, P. (2006). *Bayesian Logical Data Analysis for the Physical Sciences. A Comparative Approach with Mathematica® Support.* Cambridge: Cambridge University Press. 65

Gürtler, L., Studer, U., & Scholz, G., Eds. (2010). *Tiefensystemik. Band 1. Lebenspraxis und Theorie. Wege aus Süchtigkeit finden.* Münster: Monsenstein und Vannerdat. 18, 70

Heckhausen, H. (1989). *Motivation und Handeln.* Berlin: Springer. 32

Hildenbrand, B. (1991). *Alltag als Therapie. Ablösesprozesse Schizophrener in der psychiatrischen Übergangseinrichtung.* Bern: Hans Huber. 30

Hildenbrand, B. (1995). Professionelles Handeln im Gesundheitswesen zwischen Autonomie- und Heteronomie-Orientierung. Unveröffentlichtes Manuskript, Universität Jena. 20

Hildenbrand, B. (1996). Methodik der Einzelfallstudie: Theoretische Grundlagen, Erhebungs- und Auswertungsverfahren, vorgeführt an Fallbeispielen. Studienbrief in drei Bänden. Unveröffentlichtes Manuskript, Fernuniversität Hagen. 28

Hildenbrand, B. (1999/ 2005b). *Fallrekonstruktive Familienforschung. Anleitungen für die Praxis. 2. Auflage.* Wiesbaden: Verlag für Sozialwissenschaften. 28

Hildenbrand, B. (2005a). *Einführung in die Genogrammarbeit.* Heidelberg: Carl-Auer Systeme. 28

Jaynes, E. (2003). *Probability theory: The logic of science. Edited by G. Larry Bretthorst.* Cambridge: Cambrige University Press. 66

Kluge, S. (2000). Empirisch begründete typenbildung in der qualitativen sozialforschung. *Forum Qualitative Sozialforschung*, 1. http://www. qualitative-research.net/fqs-texte/1-00/1-00kluge-d.htm. 28

Koob, G. & LeMoal, M., Eds. (2006). *Neurobiology of addiction*. London: Academic Press. 31

Nash, M. (1997). Addicted. Why do people get hooked? *Time*, May 26, 47–52. http://www.time.com/time/magazine/article/0,9171, 986282-1,00.html. 34, 84

Oevermann, U. (1996). Theoretische Skizze einer revidierten Theorie professionalisierten Handelns. In A. Combe & W. Helsper (Eds.), *Pädagogische Professionalität: Untersuchungen zum Typus pädagogischen Handelns* (pp.70–182). Frankfurt am Main: Suhrkamp. 29

Oevermann, U. (1997). Gebildeter Fundamentalismus oder pragmatische Krisenbewältigung. Unveröffentlichtes Manuskript, korrigierte Version, Universität Frankfurt am Main. 20, 28

Oevermann, U. (2000). Die Methode der Fallrekonstruktion in der Grundlagenforschung sowie der klinischen und pädagogischen Praxis. In K. Kraimer (Ed.), *Die Fallrekonstruktion. Sinnverstehen in der sozialwissenschaftlichen Forschung* (pp. 58–156). Frankfurt am Main: Suhrkamp. 23,27

Oevermann, U., Allert, T., Konau, E., & Krambeck, J. (1979). Die Methodologie einer »objektiven Hermeneutik« und ihre allgemeine forschungslogische Bedeutung in den Sozialwissenschaften. In H.-G. Soeffner (Ed.), *Interpretative Verfahren in den Sozial- und Textwissenschaften* (pp. 352–433). Stuttgart: Metzler. 23, 65

Peciña, S., Smith, K., & Berridge, K. (2006). Hedonic hot spots in the brain. *The Neuroscientist*, 12 (6), 500–511. 31

Pólya, G. (1954/ 1990a). *Mathematics and Plausible Reasoning: Induction and Analogy in Mathematics. Vol. I*. New Jersey: Princeton University Press. 55, 66

Pólya, G. (1954/ 1990b). *Mathematics and Plausible Reasoning: Patterns of Plausible Inference: Patterns of Plausible Inference. Vol. II*. New Jersey: Princeton University Press. 55, 66

Popper, K. (1943). *Logik der Forschung. 11. Auflage 2005, herausgegeben von Herberth Keupp, Tübingen: Mohr*. Wien. 28

Revenstorf, D. (1993). *Psychotherapeutische Verfahren. Band 3: Humanistische Therapien*. Stuttgart: Kohlhammer. 20

Robinson, S., Sandstrom, S., Denenberg, V., & Palmiter, R. (2005). Distinguishing whether dopamine regulates liking, wanting, and/ or learning about rewards. *Behavioral Neuroscience*, 119, 5–15. 31, 34

Robinson, T. & Berridge, K. (1993). The neural basis of drug craving: An incentive-sensitization theory of addiction. *Brain Research Review*, 18, 247–291. 27, 31, 32

Robinson, T. & Berridge, K. (1995). The mind of an addicted brain: Neural sensitization of wanting versus liking. *Current Directions in psychological science*, 4 (3), 71–76. 31

Robinson, T. & Berridge, K. (2000). Animal models in craving research. The psychology and neurobiology of addiction: An incentive-sensitization view. *Addiction*, 95 (2), 91–117. 31

Robinson, T. & Berridge, K. (2001). Incentive-sensitization and addiction. *Addiction*, 96, 103–114. 31

Robinson, T. & Berridge, K. (2003). Addiction. *Annu. Rev. Psychol.*, 54, 25–53. 24, 31, 32

Robinson, T. & Berridge, K. (2004). Incentive-sensitization and drug »wanting«. *Psychopharmacology*, 171, 352–353. 31

Robinson, T. & Berridge, K. (2008). The incentive sensitization theory of addiction: Some current issues. *Philosophical transactions of the Royal Society B*, 363, 3137–3146. 31, 34

Scholz, G. (1992). *Vipassanā Meditation und Drogensucht. Eine Studie über den Ausstieg aus der Herrschaft der Attraktion Droge.* PhD thesis. Unveröffentlichte Dissertation, Universität Zürich. 41, 49

Schumann, H. W. (1999). *Der historische Buddha. Leben und Lehre des Gotama.* München: Diederichs. 36

Schumann, H. W. (2000). *Buddhismus. Stifter, Schulen und Systeme.* München: Diederichs Gelbe Reihe. 36

Schumann, H. W. (2001). *Handbuch Buddhismus. Die zentralen Lehren. Ursprung und Gegenwart.* München: Diederichs Gelbe Reihe. 36

Smith, K. & Berridge, K. (2007). Opioid limbic circuit for reward: Interaction between hedonic hotspots of Nucleus Accumbens and Ventral Palladium. *The Journal of Neuroscience*, 27 (7), 1594–1605. 31

Stachowske, R. (2002). *Mehrgenerationentherapie und Genogramme in der Drogenhilfe. Drogenabhängigkeit und Familiengeschichte.* Heidelberg: Asanger. 28

Studer, U. (1995). *Therapieforschung in START AGAIN: Eine Werkstattschau.* Jahresbericht des *START AGAIN* 1995, Zürich. 25

Studer, U. (1996). *Evaluation des Suchttherapiezentrums Start Again.* Technical report, Zürich. Zwischenbericht an das Bundesamt für Justiz (BAJ) vom Dezember 1996. 66

Studer, U. (1998). *Verlangen, Süchtigkeit und Tiefensystemik.* Technical report, Zürich. Evaluationsbericht an das Justizministerium (BAJ) der Schweiz, http://www.ofj.admin.ch/themen/stgb-smv/bermv/37.pdf. 18, 46, 48, 50, 52, 65, 77, 79

Studer, U. (2006). Probability theory and inference: How to draw consistent conclusions from incomplete information. *Qualitative Research in Psychology*, 3, 329–345. 66, 70

Thompson, E. (2006). Neurophenomenology and contemplative experience. In E. Clayton (Ed.), *The Oxford Handbook of Science and Religion.* Oxford: Oxford University Press. http://individual.utoronto.ca/evant/ OxfordHanbook.pdf. 85

U Ko Lay (1995). *Essence of Tipi.taka.* Igatpuri, India: V.R.I. 36

Vipassanā Research Institute, Ed. (1993). *Mahā satipaṭṭhāna Suttam.* . Igatpuri, India: V.R.I. 37, 38, 41

Vipassanā Research Institute, Ed. (2000). *Cha.t.ta San'gā yana edition of the Tipitaka. Compiled and published by Vipassanā Research Institute.* Igatpuri, India: V.R.I. http://www.tipitaka.org. 36, 37

Volkow, N., Wang, G.-J., Fowler, J., Fischman, M., Foltin, R., Abumrad, N., Gatley, S., Logan, J., Wong, C., Gifford, A., Ding, Y.-S., Hitzemann, R., & Pappas, N. (1999). Methylphenidate and cocaine have a similar in vivo potency to block dopamine transporters in the human brain. *Life Sciences*, 65 (1), PL7–PL12. 34

Wallace, D. (1998). *A Supposedly Fun Thing I'll Never Do Again: Essays and Arguments.* New York: Little Brown and Company. 21

Welter-Enderlin, R. & Hildenbrand, B. (1996). *Systemische Therapie als Begegnung.* Stuttgart: Klett-Cotta. 27

Wernet, A. (2000). *Einführung in die Interpretationstechnik der Objektiven Hermeneutik.* Opladen: Leske + Budrich. 28

Winkielman, P. & Berridge, K. (2003). Irrational wanting and subrational liking: How rudimentary motivational and affective processes shape preferences and choices. *Political Psychology*, 24 (4), 657–680. 31

Wittgenstein, L. (1963). *Tractatus logico-philosophicus = Logisch-philosophische Abhandlung (Erstveröffentlichung 1921)*. Frankfurt am Main: Suhrkamp. 35

Wyvell, C. & Berridge, K. (2000). Intra-Accumbens amphetamine increases the conditioned incentive salience of sucrose reward: Enhancement of reward »wanting« without enhanced »liking« or response reinforcement. *The Journal of Neuroscience*, 20, 8122–8130. 31

ABOUT PARIYATTI

Pariyatti is dedicated to providing affordable access to authentic teachings of the Buddha about the Dhamma theory (*pariyatti*) and practice (*paṭipatti*) of Vipassana meditation. A 501(c)(3) nonprofit charitable organization since 2002, Pariyatti is sustained by contributions from individuals who appreciate and want to share the incalculable value of the Dhamma teachings. We invite you to visit www.pariyatti.org to learn about our programs, services, and ways to support publishing and other undertakings.

Pariyatti Publishing Imprints

Vipassana Research Publications (focus on Vipassana as taught by S.N. Goenka in the tradition of Sayagyi U Ba Khin)

BPS Pariyatti Editions (selected titles from the Buddhist Publication Society, copublished by Pariyatti)

MPA Pariyatti Editions (selected titles from the Myanmar Pitaka Association, copublished by Pariyatti)

Pariyatti Digital Editions (audio and video titles, including discourses)

Pariyatti Press (classic titles returned to print and inspirational writing by contemporary authors)

Pariyatti enriches the world by

- disseminating the words of the Buddha,
- providing sustenance for the seeker's journey,
- illuminating the meditator's path.